DISPENSATIONALISM
IN A POST-MODERN WORLD

DR. BILL SHADE

DISPENSATIONALISM IN A POST-MODERN WORLD
By: Dr. Bill Shade
Illustrations By: Heather Wilson

ISBN-13: 978-1514710920

ISBN-10: 1514710927

Printed in the United States of America

Copyright © 2015 by Dr. Bill Shade

All rights reserved solely by the author. No part of this book may be reproduced in any form without the written permission of the author.

Unless otherwise indicated, Bible quotations are taken from the King James Version of the Bible

Portions of this book were taken from the WWBI course, God's Plan of the Ages. The course was authored by Dr. Bill Shade and is copyrighted by Source of Light Ministries Int. Those portions used were by permission of the copyright holder.

Visit our website at: BillShade.org

DEDICATION

This book is dedicated to the churches and friends who, by their prayers and support have, for nearly sixty years, made our ministry possible.

THANK YOU

CONTENTS:

Foreword

SECTION ONE: PRELIMINARY CONSIDERATIONS

1. Introduction 1
2. Defining Terms 9
3. Gaining Perspective 17

SECTION TWO: THE SEVEN DISPENSATIONS

4. The Dispensation of Innocence 25
5. The Dispensation of Conscience 33
6. The Dispensation of Human Government 41
7. The Dispensation of Promise .51
8. The Dispensation of Law:
   The Law Given 61
9. The Dispensation of Law:
   Three Periods Under Law 67
10. The Dispensation of Law:
    The Purpose of the Law .74
11. The Dispensation of Grace:
    Some Vital Explanations 83
12. The Dispensation of Grace:
    The Dispensation Analyzed 91
13. The Dispensation of Grace:
    The Failure – Apostasy 101
14. The Dispensation of the Kingdom:
    Reasons for the Kingdom 113
15. The Dispensation of the Kingdom:
    Analyzing the Final Dispensation 127

SECTION THREE: ADDITIONAL ISSUES AND CONSIDERATIONS

16. Making Dispensational Distinctions 139
17. Salvation in Dispensationalism 143
18. Dispensational Perspicuity 153
19. Dispensational vs. Covenant Theology 159
20. The Church Age – A Prophetic Parenthesis 167
21. Dispensational Transitions 177
22. Dispensational Principles in Matthew 183
23. Dispensational Principles in Acts 191
24. Dispensationalism: What We Can Learn 201
Appendix 207

Foreword

It has been my happy privilege to teach and preach the Word of God on four continents. I frequently ministered in Europe after the fall of communism, and have preached in villages and cities all over India. I have ministered to many countries in Africa, and in the Philippines as well as the continental USA. I have taught in Bible colleges and seminaries.

Wherever I have gone, and whatever subject I have taught, the basic framework for that teaching has been a dispensational understanding of Scripture. Whether teaching a particular book, or a subject such as Ecclesiology, Pneumatology, or Eschatology, my understanding of that subject has led me to a renewed confidence in my dispensational perspective.

I am not alone. I have found that churches and colleges all over the world hold to a basic understanding of those doctrines which Dispensationalism defines. They believe in a Pre-Tribulation Rapture for the Church, a cessationist understanding of the sign gifts, and a future conversion of the nation Israel.

However, I also discovered that while holding to the doctrinal conclusions of Dispensational Theology, my generation no longer teaches the basis for those conclusions – they do not teach Dispensationalism itself. As a result, the great doctrinal heritage received from former generations is beginning to be questioned and lost to this present generation.

All of that is exacerbated by the rise of Postmodernism which denies the very existence of the kind of metanarrative provided by a dispensational approach to Scripture. Given the present environment, I cannot think of anything more important than to re-examine our understanding of Dispensationalism. I hope that what I say in this book can contribute to this crucial discussion and that others will join that conversation as well.

SECTION ONE:
PRELIMINARY CONSIDERATIONS

CHAPTER ONE:
INTRODUCTION

We live today in what has been called a "Postmodern Era". The mind-set of Postmodernism is that there are no absolutes, no certain and reliable truths and no metanarrative to history. In other words, there is no grand, overriding plan to history - nothing that explains it, or gives it meaning or direction. To Postmoderns, human history is nothing but a scramble of unrelated, and mostly unfortunate events. As Shakespeare put it, "Life's but a walking shadow, a poor player that struts and frets his hour upon the stage and then is heard no more: it is a tale told by an idiot, full of sound and fury, signifying nothing" [1]

However, God has placed within man an innate sense that there must be, somewhere, somehow, a unifying cord, a dominate theme, a master plan that makes sense of man's journey on planet earth. When once that plan, that theme is discovered, all of the disconnected parts begin to fall into place and man sees at last a completeness in which he can rest. Suddenly, the world, and history, and life itself make sense for the first time. That is the lesson that we are learning again and again in modern day missions.

The conversion of the Mouk tribe in Papua, New Guinea became a water shed event in the way modern missions are conducted. The moment the primitive Mouk realized that all the stories they had heard from missionary Mark Zook were leading up to God's final and great redemptive act at the cross, the light of faith flared and the entire tribe embraced the Gospel message. Since that event evangelical missions have been looking at what happened on that occasion to develop a model of communicating the whole of God's Story before trying to communicate the particulars.

We miss the entire point however, if we think that laying out a broad picture that traces a plan and purpose to history is only essential for people like the Mouk. The basic problems we face today in super high tech societies are all related to the same problem. Our Postmodern society has been strongly influenced by the godless philosophy of humanism.

Humanism has its basis in evolution which attempts to explain the existence of everything apart from God. In such a system man becomes the sum total of everything and secularism is the outworking of humanism, denying the very existence of God.

Once God is denied, there are no certain answers, no purpose for living, and no final goal toward which all history is moving. There is only me, my existence, and the next moment to live for – and what better describes this generation, not only in America, but across the globe?

There is, for this generation, no grand design, no ultimate purpose, or as it is often called, no metanarrative. The word metanarrative simply means, the Big Story. The Big Story is the thread that weaves together the pieces and makes a tapestry out of the tangled threads of history and life.

In an article on Postmodernism, D. P. Teague writes, ". . . postmodern people do not believe in metanarratives. They feel that there are no grand stories which give meaning to all of life and which define what is true." [2]

Jean-Francois Lyotard (1924-1998), the postmodern philosopher, said: "Simplifying to the extreme, I define postmodern as incredulity towards metanarratives." [3]

What that means is that many in our time have given up on the idea that there is an answer to the basic questions: where did we come from, why are we here, and where are we going? But some are searching and when and if a convincing metanarrative is offered to them, there is often an exciting response of faith.

The same article cites the following example, "The magazine *Christianity Today* once ran an article by the title *"I Was a Witch."* It is the story of Kimberly Shumate and her long journey toward conversion to Christ. Concerning one particularly poignant moment in her journey, she writes of the power of the Big Story in her life:"

> "As Lisa drove me home, my mind ached as I replayed Scott's words. All the Old Testament and New Testament verses had one oddly familiar voice — one tone, one heart. I wondered, How could a book written by so many different people over the course of hundreds of years fit together perfectly as if one amazing storyteller has written the whole thing? The Holy Spirit began melting my vanity and arrogance with a power stronger than any hex, incantation, or spell I'd ever used. Suddenly, the blindfold I'd worn for almost 30 years was stripped away, and instantly I knew what I'd been searching for: it was JESUS!" [4]

What can we learn from all of this? Simply that Postmoderns have the same need for an overarching meaning to history and life as do primitive peoples like the Mouk. All of us want and need to know that there is a Grand Design, an ultimate purpose, an infinite plan that gives meaning and purpose to everything.

That is the significance of reaffirming again the Dispensational approach to the Scriptures. Dispensationalism's understanding of history can dispel or refute humanistic and hopeless ideas. Such a study demonstrates that God's predetermined plan is behind the twists and turns found in both history and sacred Scripture. God does have a purpose and an ultimate and glorious goal in human history. Once God's purposes and plan are understood, that understanding will give purpose and meaning to both the past and the future.

Dispensational study traces the dealings of God with man from Creation to the present and beyond. It establishes the Sovereign purposes of God in human affairs, man's consistent and redundant failure, and God's just and sometimes traumatic judgment, followed by His patient and persistent mercy. There are many and profound lessons to be learned, but none more important than this; God has a plan and a program which He is working out in human history. The sometimes confusing events have meaning and are moving inexorably toward God's determined end.

A dispensational approach also demonstrates as nothing else can the fact that man is sinful and will inevitably fail in any responsibility God gives him. Further, it underscores the truth that there are serious consequences to sin and failure.

Dispensational study also assures us that God will always intervene on behalf of those who have put their faith in Him. God always has a predetermined remedy for all of man's failures and the pattern of this is nowhere more clearly seen than in a study of the dispensations.

The study of the dispensations is a study in discernment. It is a study that teaches the student to discriminate. It means careful observation and critical interpretation of the text of Scripture. It means recognizing differences and identifying them. In short, it means, *rightly dividing the Word of Truth* (2 Timothy 2:15).

Discrimination leads to an awesome respect for the text. Dr. David Larsen has rightly observed that, "Hermeneutics is the science and art of correctly interpreting and explaining the text. Dispensationalism has a distinctive hermeneutical stance which sets it over against competitive systems. Dispensationalism insists on the plain, simple, natural meaning of the text, literal where possible." 5

The Dispensationalist believes that God is able to say exactly what he means. If He wants us to understand that He is talking about Israel, He says Israel. If He wants to tell us truth concerning the Church, He says Church. We do not try to second guess God. Correctly interpreting the text means discerning what the text says and accepting it, not imposing my interpretation on an unwilling and reluctant text.

A study of the dispensations also allows us to get "the big picture" in history. Why is that important? Imagine the difficulty of trying to put together a 5,000-piece jigsaw puzzle if you had all the pieces, but did not have the box with the completed picture on it. You could examine all the details with as much care and precision as possible, but it would be very difficult to figure out how the pieces relate to one another and how each one fits into the overall intended result.

And even if you were to successfully assemble several groups of pieces scattered around the picture by matching colors and patterns, it would still be very difficult to figure out how these groups fit together when they don't seem to match up in any obvious way. It wouldn't take very long for most people to resign themselves to defeat.

Unfortunately, this is the way many try to understand the Bible - spending a lot of time looking at the details, but without having the big picture as a point of reference. They read the same familiar passages over and over, realizing that they must fit together in some way, but find making it fit daunting and perplexing.

Or going back to the puzzle analogy, some have even concluded that the pieces don't really fit at all to form a single picture, but are really just parts of many different, unrelated pictures. This can make it virtually impossible to understand and appreciate the fact that God has a plan that He has been sovereignly and faithfully executing throughout history.

There is an ancient Indian proverb, later set to poetry, which illustrates well the basic problem. It is the proverb of Six Blind Men and the Elephant. I include it here so that you can sense, with those blind men, their dilemma and ours.

The Blind Men and the Elephant

It was six men of Indostan
To learning much inclined,
Who went to see the Elephant
(Though all of them were blind),
That each by observation
Might satisfy his mind.

The *First* approached the Elephant,
And happening to fall
Against his broad and sturdy side,
At once began to bawl:
"God bless me! but the Elephant
Is very like a WALL!"

The *Second*, feeling of the tusk,
Cried, "Ho, what have we here,
So very round and smooth and sharp?
To me 'tis mighty clear
This wonder of an Elephant
Is very like a SPEAR!"

The *Third* approached the animal,
And happening to take
The squirming trunk within his hands,
Thus boldly up and spake:
"I see," quoth he, "the Elephant
Is very like a SNAKE!"

> The *Fourth* reached out an eager hand,
> And felt about the knee
> "What most this wondrous beast is like
> Is mighty plain," quoth he:
> "'Tis clear enough the Elephant
> Is very like a TREE!"
>
> The *Fifth*, who chanced to touch the ear,
> Said: "E'en the blindest man
> Can tell what this resembles most;
> Deny the fact who can,
> This marvel of an Elephant
> Is very like a FAN!"
>
> The *Sixth* no sooner had begun
> About the beast to grope,
> Than seizing on the swinging tail
> That fell within his scope,
> "I see," quoth he, "the Elephant
> Is very like a ROPE!"
>
> And so these men of Indostan
> Disputed loud and long,
> Each in his own opinion
> Exceeding stiff and strong,
> Though each was partly in the right,
> And all were in the wrong! 6

So much of our Bible study follows the same erroneous pattern as is illustrated by the parable. We examine with great attention certain parts of the Scripture and draw conclusions, without making reference to the whole. What a study of the dispensations does is to make us aware of the whole.

The study takes us from the creation to the consummation and demonstrates how God's sovereign plan is working out despite man's persistent failures. A study of the dispensations provides a sense of man's failure and God's wisdom, judgment, mercy and grace like no other study I know. A study of the dispensations provides what this generation needs so desperately, a satisfying metanarrative . . . so let's find it in the pages of God's divine revelation.

CHAPTER TWO:
DEFINING TERMS

Dispensation is the translation of the Greek word, *oikonomia,* which means the management, arrangement, stewardship or administration of the affairs of the household. As it is used in the Scriptures, it means the order or arrangement (management) of God's house. It points to that plan or arrangement by which God deals with man in general, or with certain groups of men in particular, during a certain period of time.

There are those who have criticized Dispensationalists for saying that the term *oikonomia,* has to do with certain periods of time. They insist that the word means only "stewardship" and has nothing to do with time periods. But the argument is puerile. We live in a space/time continuum and therefore any stewardship must engage a certain part of that time continuum. So when we say that a dispensation is the way God manages His people during a particular period, we are simply recognizing the fact that all that happens, happens in time and can be viewed epically.

Dispensationalism is deemed such an important hermeneutical position that certain denominations, and mission agencies have incorporated it into their doctrinal statements. Well known evangelical mission Biblical Ministries Worldwide (BMW), is an example as is the church fellowship of IFCA.

When a dispensational approach to Scripture is taken, it become extremely clear that God has carried out distinctive programs with different groups of people and that every plan and purpose of God with whatever group or entity will be completely fulfilled and satisfied.

Dispensationalism recognizes a distinct difference between God's plan and purpose with Israel and His plan and purpose with the Church. Dispensationalists see no evidence that the Church began with Adam or that Israel was merely God's expression of the Church during the former age. In fact, Dr. John MacArthur sums it up succinctly when he says, "Dispensationalism in one sentence – it is the distinction between Israel and the Church." [1]

Israel has a specific beginning and so did the Church. Israel began with the call of Abraham and the Church began with the coming of the Holy Spirit on the Day of Pentecost. Failing to observe these distinctions, leads to confusion in interpretations on such essential matters as Law and Grace and especially God future program with the Church and Israel.

Dispensationalists believe that while God's purpose of Redemption by Grace through Faith has been consistent from the beginning, His means of testing man has varied, and there has been a progressive series of tests in each new period.

Through the centuries, men of God have attempted to define the Dispensations beginning with the first century after the Apostles. Dr. Thomas Ice writes, "Crude, but clear, schemes of ages and dispensations are found in ante-Nicene fathers such as Justin Martyr (110-165), Irenaeus (130-200), Tertullian (160-220), Methodius (311), and Victorinus of Petau (304)." [2]

Bible instructor, Larry V. Crutchfield, of Baumholder, West Germany, writes, "The early Fathers viewed God's dealings with His people in dispensational terms. . . . In every major area of importance in the early church one finds rudimentary features of Dispensationalism that bear a striking resemblance to their contemporary offspring." [3]

While all Scriptural study suffered during the dark ages of Rome's domination, as the light of the Reformation began to dawn new attempts were made to understand the plan of God through Scripture and in 1687, Pierre Poiret developed a complete dispensational scheme in his six volume work, *The Divine Economy*. [4]

In a few short years Isaac Watts (1674-1748), the famous theologian and hymn writer, wrote about dispensations in a forty-page essay entitled "The Harmony of all the Religions which God ever Prescribed to Men and all his Dispensations towards them." [5]

In 1699, John Edwards published, *A Complete History or Survey of All the Dispensations,* in two volumes, totaling about 790 pages, and the first systematic expression of Dispensationalism was formulated by J. N. Darby sometime during the late 1820s and 1830s in the British Isles.

All of these attempts differed to some extent but each made its own contribution until C. I. Scofield, and others who labored with him, established basically the seven dispensational periods that we are most familiar with today.

Each new attempt refined our understanding of how to identify dispensations and what constitutes a biblical dispensation. And that leads to the obvious question, what does constitute a biblical dispensation? Or to ask the question in another way, what distinguishing characteristics allow for a certain period of time to be identified as a genuine dispensation? I would argue that there are six — six distinguishing marks or features apart from which we cannot truly identify a particular period as a true dispensation.

For the sake of memory, I have used words beginning with the letter "R" to identify them.

1. **Responsibility:** Since it is commonly agreed that a dispensation is a period of testing, there must of necessity then be an identifiable "Test" or responsibility — something which men are expected to do. For instance, in the first dispensation called Innocence, the

responsibility of the couple was to "dress and keep" the garden in which the LORD God had placed them. In the Dispensation of Human Government man's responsibility was to govern as the agent of God, or rule for God. Whatever the responsibility might be however, unless there is a clear indication of something for which man will be held accountable, we cannot rightly identify that period as a true dispensation.

2. **Restriction:** Not only does each dispensation constitute a defined responsibility, but along with that responsibility God will have laid down certain restrictions. Once again, in the first dispensation the restriction was clearly stated, *Of every tree of the garden thou mayest freely eat: But of the tree of the knowledge of good and evil, thou shalt not eat of it: for in the day that thou eatest thereof thou shalt surely die.* — Restriction! Along with new revelation which defined new responsibility, came boundaries or restrictions. In the second dispensation these are not defined since man's Responsibility is to "do well" according to his conscience, and hence conscience itself becomes the restricting factor. Obviously this idea can be traced into the later dispensational periods as well, but with every true dispensation (stewardship) there is both a Responsibility and certain Restrictions.

3. **Relationship:** In any period which can be identified as a true dispensation there will be a discernible relationship adjustment. The question to ask is, "How does man relate to God in this period that differs from former times?" Obviously Adam and Eve enjoyed direct unbroken fellowship with God during the Dispensation of Innocence. Under Conscience, we see men acting as their own priest, each individually bringing his offering or sacrifice. In the next dispensation, the Dispensation of Human Government, the relationship seems to rest upon the national head. In the next dispensation (Promise), the family patriarch acted as the family priest as well, and under the Mosaic Law

"Relationship" is exercised through the intermediary of the Aaronic Priesthood. But in each case there is a discernible shift in the way man relates or comes to God during that period and that forms another criteria for judging the period a true dispensation.

4. **Ruination:** The next "R" word represents the recurring feature of each dispensation, the failure of man, invariably at the very place where he is being tested. Presbyterian Dr. Donald Grey Barnhouse said, "Sometimes a student may say, 'I failed that test because the teacher asked the wrong questions.' By the time God has finished His Dispensational testing of man it will be evident that man will fail no matter what the question."[6] In each period, therefore, that constitutes a true dispensation, we will be able to discern a failure at the very point of Responsibility and/or Restriction.

5. **Reckoning:** This word basically means, "to call into account." That is indeed how it is used here. At the close of every true dispensational period there will be a judgment upon the failure of man. In the first dispensation, that judgment involved not only expulsion from the garden, but changes in relationships — man to woman, man to the earth, and a host of other things. In the second dispensation, man's horrific failure to let his conscience direct him ended in the destruction of the earth through a universal flood. In the third dispensation, man's governmental mismanagement and rebellion was met with the division of tongues at Babel and the dispersion of the nations.

When Abraham's descendants forgot the Promises and settled down comfortably in Egypt, judgment came in the form of tyrannical slavery under a genocidal Pharaoh. In the Dispensation of Law, various judgments marked the three distinct periods of this dispensation, but the final Reckoning for a broken Law fell upon the Savior Himself at the Cross. During the present Dispensation of Grace, man's responsibility is to "repent and believe the gospel." Since this dispensation once again tests all men, all are held responsible and God's reckoning with an apostate and unbelieving world will come during the seven years of Great Tribulation following the Rapture of the Church. Finally, in the Dispensation of the Kingdom, man's final failure and rebellion will end in the complete destruction of the present heaven and earth and a new heaven and earth wherein will dwell righteousness. Reckoning or judgment is a necessary feature in discerning a period to be a true dispensation.

6. **Remedy:** Finally, the word Remedy describes God's gracious intervention at the end of each of man's failures. Each time man fails, God judges, but God also provides a path of mercy which leads to greater things. God graciously expelled man from the garden to prevent him from eating of the tree of life and becoming forever fixed in his sinful and fallen condition. For the flood, He provided the Ark. After the debacle at Babel, He called Abraham. After the cross, He extended grace and forgiveness, and after man's final failure in His Millennial Kingdom, He will provide a New Heaven and a New Earth.

Every dispensation is marked with these six distinguishing features and thus the designation of a particular period as a true dispensation (stewardship) is not arbitrary, but defined by certain criteria. By applying these criteria to our study, we can clearly identify the seven dispensations that we will look at as we move forward.

There is yet one other critical idea here which must not be missed. The very idea of a series of biblical dispensations implies progression of both revelation and duty. Thus the Dispensationalist believes in a progress of doctrinal revelation and moral responsibility within the Scriptures. Each new Responsibility, every new Restriction, each adjusted Relationship revealed something more of God – His nature, His holiness, and His grace. With this in mind, I invite you to begin our exploration of God's "Big Story."

CHAPTER THREE:
GAINING PERSPECTIVE

Have you ever entered the wrong house by accident? I was visiting relatives in New York City and got into the wrong apartment house. There were three apartment buildings clustered together, all exactly alike. I rode up and down the elevator trying to find the right apartment when all the while I was in the wrong building.

Such experiences are amusing because they are of little consequence. However, when we are confused in matters pertaining to God's Word, it is not amusing because the consequences are eternal.

The Bible teaches us to distinguish things that differ. In the very beginning, God separated the light from the darkness. He said of His priests, *And they shall teach my people the difference between the holy and profane, and cause them to discern between the unclean and the clean* (Ezekiel 44:23). Discernment and critical thinking are essential to biblical analysis.

Jesus was critical of the leaders in His day for their lack of ability to distinguish and discern. *He answered and said unto them, When it is evening, ye say, It will be fair weather: for the sky is red. And in the morning, It will be foul weather today: for the sky is red and* *lowering. O ye hypocrites, ye can discern the face of the sky; but can ye not discern the signs of the times (*Matthew 16:2, 3)?

God is all about distinguishing things that differ and the study of the dispensations is an exercise in distinguishing God's changing administrations as He progressively reveals Himself and His ways to man.

Probably the key verse in any dispensational study is 2 Timothy 2:15. *Study to show thyself approved unto God, a workman that needeth not to be ashamed, rightly dividing the word of truth.* The phrase *rightly dividing* is from the Greek **orthotomeo,** which means literally to cut a straight line. It would describe what a tent maker would do as he cut out from a large canvas the particular pieces to form the tent. Paul's trade was that of a tent maker and he borrowed a word from that background to make his point.

There is clear intimation here that the Bible has certain proper divisions. It also appears that we may "divide" the Word of Truth rightly as a result of careful study. There is a further assumption in this verse that not every Christian can do this, and that some even divide it wrongly.

As we saw in the last chapter, the word "dispensation" in the New Testament is translated from the Greek word, **oikonomia,** which means the management, arrangement, and administration of the affairs of the household. As it is used scripturally, it means the order or arrangement (management) of God's house (the world). It points to that plan or arrangement by which God deals with man, or a specific group of men, during a certain period of time.

It may be observed that everyone who honestly studies the Scripture, is to some degree a Dispensationalist. Whether you have studied the dispensational pattern of Scripture or not, you already distinguish between the Old Testament and the New. When you read of man's pristine condition in the Garden of Eden, it is not difficult to see that everything changed after he had fallen into sin and you make distinctions about God's dealing with him before and after the Fall.

Any reader of the books of Romans or Galatians, must certainly become aware that there is a vast difference between Law and Grace. In fact you are introduced to that fact as early as the first chapter of John's Gospel, where we read, *The law was given by Moses, but grace and truth came by Jesus Christ* (John 1:17).

And if you read the Scripture taking the plain literal sense of the words, you cannot help seeing a vast difference take place on the earth when Christ returns to reign with His saints for a thousand years as we are clearly told He will do (Isaiah 11, 12; Revelation 19).

If you are still with me, you have already distinguished five periods where man's situation and God's administration changes. You are already a four or five point Dispensationalist.

Saint Augustine is credited with the following words of wisdom, "Distinguish the ages, and the Scriptures will harmonize." It is unfortunate for the Church that Augustine failed to heed his own advice. Because he failed to make those distinctions, especially between God's purposes for Israel and for the Church, he framed the Church as a "Theocratic Kingdom" intended to rule over the earth. Having done so, he put the Church on a course that involved her in the political intrigues of the next thousand years and blinded her to her heavenly calling.

Jesus' words recorded by John in chapter four have unmistakable dispensational implications. *Jesus saith unto her, Woman, believe me, the hour cometh, when ye shall neither in this mountain, nor yet at Jerusalem, worship the Father. Ye worship ye know not what: we know what we worship: for salvation is of the Jews. But the hour cometh, and now is, when the true worshippers shall worship the Father in spirit and in truth: for the Father seeketh such to worship him* (John 4:21-23).

Jesus' reference to *the hour* is certainly not to a literal hour of sixty minutes, but a certain period of time during which God does things in a certain way. Isn't it obvious, that Jesus is saying that a new dispensation is about to begin in which certain requirements and relationships of the former period will be replaced by new ones? There is also a strong implication here of a progress of revelation – both ideas are central to dispensational thought.

Or consider Jesus' words in Matthew 9 (repeated in all of the synoptic Gospels): *No man putteth a piece of new cloth unto an old garment, for that which is put in to fill it up taketh from the garment, and the rent is made worse. Neither do men put new wine into old bottles: else the bottles break, and the wine runneth out, and the bottles perish: but they put new wine into new bottles, and both are preserved* (Matthew 9:16, 17)

It could hardly be clearer that Jesus is alerting His followers that God is about to make a paradigm shift in His dealings with man. In this instance, the old garment and the old wine bottle both referred to Israel and as clear as words can be Jesus is telling us that what He is about to do is going to be a completely new thing. The New Testament Church is not an extension of Israel – it is not a patched up garment or an old bottle full of new wine. It is rather, a wholly new entity.

God never changes, but His dealings with man do change. Because that is true, you do not make a pilgrimage to Jerusalem each year to worship God as clearly commanded in a former dispensation (Deuteronomy 12:1-14; 16:13-16; Zechariah 14:16-17). A new dispensation has begun in which the requirements and relationships of the former period have been replaced by new ones.

So Dispensationalism aids us in distinguishing the various purposes of God during the changing periods of the biblical record. Dr. A.T. Pierson used to compare the divisions of Scripture to his old-fashioned, cubbyhole desk. "When things are piled up on the desk, there is confusion, but when I separate them and put them in their proper cubbyhole, order and harmony exist." [1]

I believe God wants "harmony to exist" in our reading and understanding of the Scripture, and therefore it is of utmost importance that we learn to, *rightly divide the word of truth.*

KEY TO THE DISPENSATIONAL CHART

Included in this book is a dispensational chart. It is the easiest and best method devised to visualize the seven great dispensations of God's dealing with man. Before we study the chart, however, there is one question which needs to be answered. Why have there been dispensations or varying methods in God's dealings with man?

Each dispensation involves a test. At first, these tests were simple, such as the test given to our first parents in *the Garden of Eden*. However, as God's progressive revelation of Himself increased, God tested man accordingly and in progressive steps. This has always been God's method. Added knowledge brings added responsibility. Through successive dispensations, God revealed a little more of Himself to man and required man to walk by the light of each new revelation.

In each dispensation or testing, man has failed. However, God was not taken by surprise by man's failure (Acts 15:18); God already knew that man would fail although man has always been convinced that he can succeed. Through man's failure, God taught that man is completely sinful, depraved, and helpless in himself. Man cannot please God, even if he wants to do so (Romans 8:7-8).

There is another thing we should not overlook: the number "seven" is important because numbers often have significance in Scripture and "seven" signifies completeness. Once God has dealt with man through seven periods of responsibility, He will have exhausted the possibilities of testing man and will have accomplished a complete work (Ecclesiastes 3:14).

As we said before, sometimes after a test you may think, "Well, if the teacher had just asked different questions or if I had more time, I could have passed." God's seven great tests will demonstrate that man could not pass, no matter what the test.

Now look at the Chart inserted in the book. First, note that the chart is very simple. Very little has been included in this chart other than the dispensations themselves.

Secondly, the seven dispensations are named at the top of the chart reading from left to right as follows: **1. INNOCENCE, 2. CONSCIENCE, 3. HUMAN GOVERNMENT, 4. PROMISE, 5. LAW, 6. GRACE, 7. KINGDOM**. These dispensations are divided by vertical lines between which the name of the dispensation appears.

Thirdly, you will see that at the left side of the chart, there are six words: **Responsibility, Restriction, Relationship, Ruination, Reckoning, and Remedy.** These words will analyze each dispensation from its beginning to its ending in God's gracious intervention noted by the word "Remedy."

If you read directly across the chart from left to right, the verses for each heading will appear under each succeeding dispensation. For instance, the Bible reference for **Responsibility**, under the Dispensation of **Innocence**, is Genesis 2:15. Under **Conscience**, the reference for **Responsibility** is Genesis 4:7. Under **Human Government,** the reference is Genesis 9:1, 6. Under **Promise**, the reference is Genesis 12:1-3. Under **Law**, the reference is Exodus 19:5; and Deuteronomy 4:1-2. Under **Grace**, the reference is John 3:16. And under **Kingdom**, the reference is Zechariah 14:16-17. Each of the six analytical words (**Responsibility, Restriction, Relationship, Ruination, Reckoning, and Remedy**) is handled in the same way.

Finally, notice that the half circles at each end of the chart represent eternity. The line running through the center left to right from one half circle to the other is a **"Time-Line"**. The other distinctive features will be addressed as we move along in our study.

We should now be completely ready to begin walking that Time-Line and exploring God's Big Story.

SECTION TWO:
THE SEVEN DISPENSATIONS

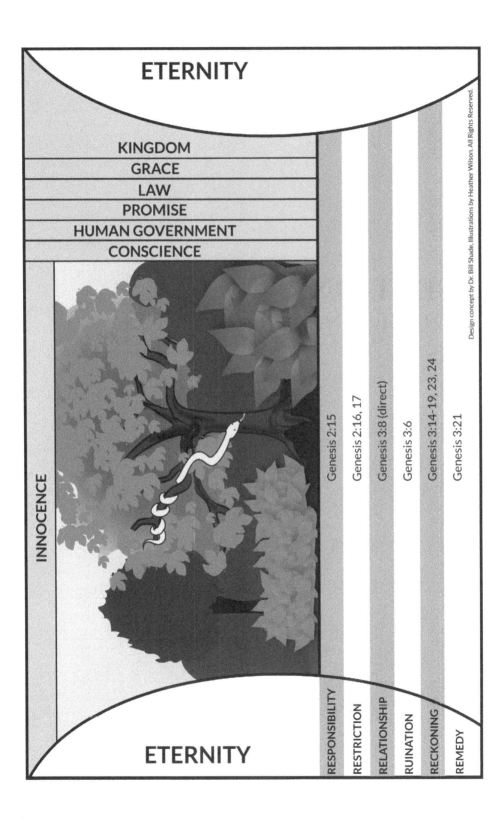

CHAPTER FOUR:
THE DISPENSATION OF INNOCENCE

We call the first Dispensation, the *Dispensation of Innocence*. Dr. Showers likes to call this "The Dispensation of an Unconfirmed Favorable Disposition." 1

I get the point, but I prefer to follow the precedent of classical Dispensationalists and just refer to it as they did. There is, of course a reason for naming it Innocence and we need to understand what it is.

Adam was created without sin and until his Fall, he was pure and unaffected by anything evil. The theological description for Adam's condition is *Innocence*. Now, please notice I did not say that Adam was righteous. There is a vast difference between being innocent and being righteous.

The "Second Adam", Jesus Christ, was also free from evil - but he was righteous as well. What is the difference? The dictionary says, "Innocent is a negative word, expressing less than righteous upright, or virtuous, which imply knowledge of good and evil, with free choice of the good. A little child or a lamb is innocent; a tried and faithful man is righteous." That is the point.

Adam was innocent because (1) he lacked the consciousness of moral values (that which constitutes an action as either right or wrong, good or evil) and (2) he was untried; he had never been tested. Thus his only virtue, "innocence", was a purely negative quality existing as a result of his creation rather than his personal goodness.

By way of contrast, Jesus Christ was the tried and faithful Man, having met the tempter with eyes open and successfully putting him to flight. He is indeed *Jesus Christ the Righteous* (1 John 2:1). Had Adam succeeded he would have become righteous. The first dispensation is the sad story that will be repeated again and again - Adam did not succeed: He failed!

The scriptural background for this dispensation is found in Genesis chapters 1-3. Of course, this is the Divine record of creation. Our culture has been plagued by the outworn and completely disproved theory of evolution. As many have observed; The theory that the world and all that is in it came about of its own accord by a mysterious process which we have pleased to call evolution is about as probable as a complete and unabridged dictionary resulting from an explosion in a print shop. The obvious fact is that design demands a Designer and this universe is characterized by unfathomable design. The answer to Darwinianism is found for the believer in Hebrews 11:3.

As we examine the account, Adam's innocent condition may be seen in three ways: First, by the name of the tree involved (Genesis 2:16, 17). It was the tree of *the knowledge of good and evil* which God wisely and graciously sought to withhold from man; therefore, it was obviously this very knowledge (i.e. of moral values) which man lacked. We call someone who lacks the understanding of right and wrong innocent.

Secondly, Adam's condition of innocence may be seen by his attitude toward his nakedness; *And they were both naked, the man and his wife, and were not ashamed* (Genesis 2:25). Again, we can relate this attitude to that of a little child, who loves nothing better than to go streaking through a crowd with nothing on at all.

As soon as Adam received a moral conscience, the first thing he wanted was a covering for his body. Nudity, whether complete or in part, is shameful and sinful (Exodus 32:25; Leviticus 20:17, 23, 24; Lamentations 1:8; Revelation 3:18). The reason for the lack of shame among many who practice and promote nudity today is not innocence, but a seared conscience (1Timothy 4:2).

Finally, we can discern Adam's innocence by the nature of the test God gave him (Genesis 2:16, 17). God's requirement was a simple command with no moral explanations. It is the way we deal with small children - or perhaps it would be better said, that it is the way we should deal with small children.

One of the most ridiculous and unproductive phenomena of our time is the parent who is trying to reason a small child out of doing something he wants to do. It usually ends in frustration for both the parent and child until little Johnnie gets his way. You don't reason with small children – you require simple obedience. As my father was prone to say, "The best reason for you to do what I told you to do, is because I told you to do it." That was reason enough.

God obviously acted toward Adam the way we should with a child. He gave him a simple command and followed it with a penalty if not obeyed, thus showing us again that Adam was in a state of innocence.

At the beginning of this chapter there is a copy of that portion of the Dispensational Chart that covers this dispensation. As we walk through the analysis of the dispensation, keep the chart clearly before you and follow by referring to the six analytical words found in the preceding chapter.

RESPONSIBILITY
Man's responsibility in this first dispensation was easy and enjoyable. He had only to dress and keep a garden which had no weeds, no thorns, and in which everything good grew of itself. It was a pleasant and profitable way for man to spend his time.

He could enjoy the fruits and flowers, pruning their branches and trimming their leaves, while walking among God's animal creatures in perfect bliss and peace (Genesis 2:15).

RELATIONSHIP
In such an environment, man walked with God. His relationship with God was direct, unbroken by sin. Under Grace we are again brought into close fellowship with God (1 John 1:3), but now it is only through the Blood which cleanses us from sin (1 John 1:7). In a spiritual sense we too can "walk with God", but Adam literally walked with his Creator.

RESTRICTION
Man's restriction was a simple demand for obedience (Genesis 2:16, 17). God said, *Thou shalt not eat thereof.* Notice how Eve made the mistake of adding to God's Word when she said, *God hath said, 'Ye shall not eat of it, neither shall ye touch it'*(Genesis 3:3).

Eve also misstated the penalty. God had said, *for in the day that thou eatest thereof thou shalt surely die,* (or literally, "dying, thou shalt die"). Eve said, *Thou shalt not eat of It . . . lest ye die,* as though there were some question about the penalty that would be enacted. We may learn from Eve that God's Word is meant to be understood in its plain and literal sense. It means what it says. In the day they ate, they were separated from God, which is spiritual death (Ephesians 2:1-13), and they began that process of bodily deterioration which separates the soul and spirit from the flesh in physical death. Dying, they most surely died!

RUINATION
Man's ruination was brought about by a three-fold lust: (1) The lust of the flesh - *when the woman saw that the tree was good for food,* (2) The lust of the eyes - *and that it was pleasant to the eyes,* and (3) The pride of life - *and a tree to be desired to make one wise, she took of the fruit thereof and did eat, and gave also to her husband with her; and he did eat.*

The harmony and continuity of Scripture is remarkable. We turn to the New Testament book of 1 John and find him telling us, *For all that is in the world, the lust of the flesh, and the lust of the eyes, and the pride of life, is not of the Father, but is of the world. And the world passeth away, and the lust thereof: but he that doeth the will of God abideth forever* (1 John 2:16, 17).

RECKONING

In God's RECKONING with man (that is, holding him accountable for his disobedience and failure), many changes took place. Remember, God always deals with sin; sooner or later there is a reckoning. He may not settle His accounts today, or tomorrow, but a judgment is coming.

(a) The serpent was changed (Genesis 3:14, 15).

(b) The woman was changed (Genesis 3:16).

(c) The earth was changed (Genesis 3:17, 18).

(d) Man's work was changed (Genesis 3:19).

(e) Man's habitation and relation to God was changed (Genesis 3: 23, 24).

In addition to all of this, it soon became evident that man's nature was also changed.

REMEDY

What was God's answer to man's flagrant and willful disobedience? Was God unprepared? Was He surprised by the ingratitude and rebellion of the creature He had made? No, God had preceded man and was prepared for his failure. We may disappoint Him, but we never take Him by surprise (Acts 15:18).

God was just in judging man's sin, but God is also love, so God made provision for man (Genesis 3:21). Note that man had tried to make provision for himself (Genesis 3:7). The fig leaves were man's first attempt to make himself presentable and acceptable to God by his own efforts.

God completely disregarded man's efforts and made them *coats of skins*. He was teaching Adam (and us), two lessons: (1) without the shedding of blood, there is no covering for sin (skins are the result of the sacrifice of an animal) and (2) only God can provide a covering (or an atonement) for man (see Isaiah 64:6; Zechariah 3:1-4; Matthew 22:11-13; Revelation 19:8).

This was God's immediate REMEDY for Adam, and it is the first picture pointing to Calvary in the Bible. God also promised an ultimate REMEDY (Genesis 3:15) in the Seed of the woman - Jesus Christ (Genesis 3:15; Galatians 3:16). Jesus is the second Adam and the Head of the New Creation, just as Adam was head of the old. The Scripture sets them in contrast in the following ways:

(a) In Adam all die (1 Corinthians 15:22).
In Christ all are made alive (1 Corinthians 15:22).

(b) In Adam all are lost (John 3:6).
In Christ all are "born again" and saved (John 1:12, 13).

(c) In Adam all have sinned (Romans 5:12, 19).
In Christ all have obtained perfect righteousness (2 Corinthians 5:21).

(d) In Adam Paradise was lost (Genesis 3:23, 24).
In Christ Paradise is regained (Revelation 20:6; 21:1-4; 22:1-5).

Summing up the Dispensation of Innocence, there are some profound lessons we can learn. We are a fallen race and in need of redemption. Jesus illustrated that best when he confronted the man, Nicodemus. Nicodemus was a good man, "In Adam"; he needed to be born again into God's new creation, "In Christ"(2 Corinthians 5:17). That fact should lead us to ask ourselves honestly, "Am I in Adam or am I in Christ?"

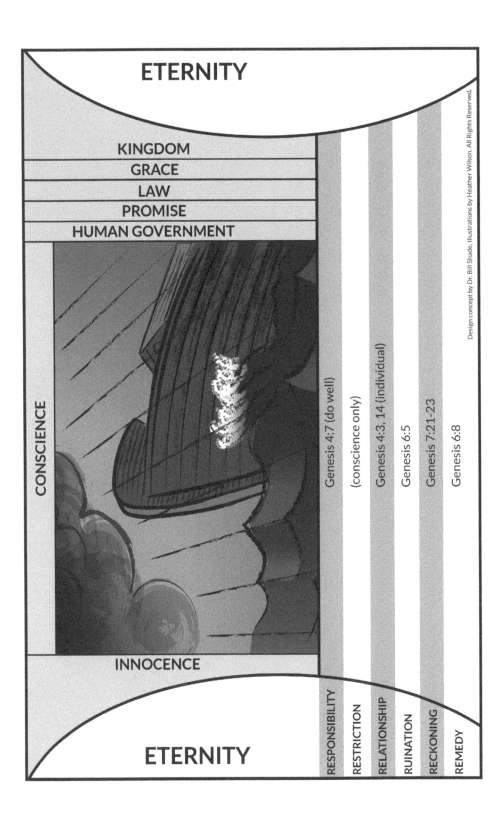

CHAPTER FIVE:
THE DISPENSATION OF CONSCIENCE

"Let your conscience be your guide." This little piece of advice has been given many times and is usually supposed to be very excellent counsel. Whether or not man's conscience is a reliable guide, and how far it can be trusted, will be seen as we look at the second dispensation. And that brings us to another question – exactly what is conscience?

We learned in the last chapter that as originally created, man was sinless and innocent. In his primal purity, he walked with God in unbroken fellowship and enjoyed the wonders of God's "very good" creation.

In his innocence he was unable to make distinctions between good and evil, so God gave him a simple command to obey, without any moral attachments, to test him in his innocent state. In the ways and wisdom of God, this very test involved the question of man's right to moral knowledge found in, *the tree of the knowledge of good and evil*. By eating of the fruit, man not only became a sinner (by disobeying God), but he also became, at the same time, a morally responsible individual (by gaining the knowledge of good and evil).

And that is precisely what conscience is. According to definition, conscience is the faculty by which distinctions are made between right and wrong in conduct and character. Webster, in his Complete Dictionary (1828) defined conscience as; "Internal or self-knowledge, or judgment of right and wrong; or the faculty, power or principle within us, which decides on the lawfulness or unlawfulness of our own actions and affections, and instantly approves or condemns them." Further, he went on to say, "The conscience manifests itself in the feeling of obligation we experience, which precedes, attends and follows our actions."[1]

And that is precisely what Adam found happened when eating the forbidden fruit. He could no longer be said to be innocent. He was both guilty of sin (thus losing his purity) and intelligent toward moral values (thus becoming possessed of a conscience).

This knowledge of good and evil – this distinction between right and wrong – placed man on an altogether different footing before God. And since man was on a different footing before God, he must be tested on the basis of this change. Since man now possessed the knowledge of good and evil, he became responsible to do good, that is, to follow the dictates of his newly acquired knowledge of good and evil and do what was right.

If man had been weak in the first Dispensation, he was worse off now. He was positively sinful. He possessed a sinful nature.

In Genesis 1:26, the God-Head took council together and said, *Let us make man in our own image, after our likeness . . . and so, God created man in his own image.* But when man fell from his original purity, that image was effaced. God, describing the effects upon man said, *the heart is deceitful above all things and desperately wicked: who can know it* (Jeremiah 17:9)?

Man's sinfulness was not simply an "act," but a "state." Furthermore, man could not help but impart his sinful nature to his posterity. When Adam begat a son, he begat him *in his own likeness, after his image* (Genesis 5:1-3).

This is the truth which the Psalmist conveyed centuries later in the words, *Behold, I was shapen in iniquity; and in sin did my mother conceive me* (Psalm 51:5). It is the truth of Romans 5:19, *by one man's* (Adam's), *disobedience many were made sinners.* It is the thing which caused Paul to say, *I know that in me (that is, in my flesh) dwelleth no good thing* (Romans 7:18). So man began the second dispensation, not only responsible to do the good he now knew, but unable (as we shall see) to do it because of a perverted and sinful nature received from Adam, the father of us all.

Furthermore, conscience itself was vulnerable. If it cried out too loudly, man found that he could silence it by building a barricade of excuses for his wrong deeds, against which his conscience could not prevail. He learned very early that habit, so prevalent among us today, to always be the "victim" and blame his misdeeds upon someone or something else.

Also, according to Scripture, conscience could become "*seared*" (1Timothy 4:2). The picture is that of a hot iron being placed against the flesh. The pain is intense at the first, but becomes less and less as the skin is numbed until it is past feeling (Ephesians 4:19).

This explains why people can sometimes live in flagrant sin and never have a sleepless night, never a prick of conscience. The sharp prick of conscience has been neutralized by frequent rationalization (excuse making).

Thus conscience tends to orient itself with the accepted standards of those around us, regardless of how wrong these may be, instead of holding to the absolute standard of right and wrong. We lose our discernment, and conscience fails to be a deterrent to sin as long as the sin is generally accepted. Like water, conscience seeks the lowest level and hence is no guide at all.

As we analyze the Dispensation of Conscience, please refer again to the Chart found at the beginning of this chapter.

RESPONSIBILITY
Hardly had the Dispensation of Conscience gotten under way when difficulty appeared. Again it was man's proud desire to prove himself acceptable to God by what his own hands could produce. Cain brought an offering of the fruit of the ground which he had labored over, while Abel offered, the firstlings of the flock, a blood offering made according to the example given by God in providing the *coats of skin*s for Adam and Eve. As a result, Scripture describes Abel's offering as being made in faith (Hebrews 11:4), while Cain offered according to his own will (Colossians 2:23).

God explained to Cain what He required, in Genesis 4:7. *If thou doest well shalt thou not be accepted?* To "do well" was simply to act in faith and according to the right principles to which Cain's own conscience now witnessed. God had demonstrated what He required in making a blood sacrifice for Adam, and there is every reason to believe that Adam followed God's example. But Cain refused to do that, and in this he set the pattern for those who followed him. Instead, he refused God's gracious appeal, took his anger out on his brother, and committed the first murder by killing Abel.

RESTRICTION
Notice that there is no verse listed on the chart in this dispensation across from Restriction. That is because there was no definite restriction placed upon man. That was required by the very nature of the test. If man was to be tested under the responsibility to do the right thing as directed by his conscience, then conscience alone must provide any restrictions which were necessary.

It was not a test to see if man could follow a set of rules – this would come later. This period of testing involved man's moral knowledge, whether man would do the thing he knew was right and refuse the thing he knew was wrong, as directed by his conscience. By failing, man showed that what he lacked was not knowledge of right and wrong, good and evil, but the ability and will to "do well."

RELATIONSHIP

Man's relationship to God was an individual matter, as will be seen by the verses on the chart. This is important, for as we go along we will see that this, too, changed in later dispensations. Man was individually responsible and was dealt with individually. *Thou hast driven me out this day from. . . thy face* (Genesis 4:14), indicated the breakdown in Cain's relationship with God. Obviously before his rebellion, he had known some sense of God's presence. Now that was to be forever lost and Cain goes off into an exile from God from which the human race has never returned. As always, this was Cain's fault - not God's.

RUINATION

The ruination of man in this dispensation demonstrates perfectly just how corrupt man's conscience can get, God's description is striking: *Every imagination of the thoughts of his heart was only evil continually* (Genesis 6:5). *Every . . . only . . . continually,* what else could be said? The failure was total, absolute, and irremediable.

Man's failure to "do well" under the dictates of his conscience ended in a prevailing evil so deep and extensive that God would intervene and destroy everything that moved and breathed upon the earth. Not only so, but the condition would become a gross picture of that condition which will precede the second glorious coming of Jesus Christ (Matthew 24:37).

RECKONING

The result was inevitable. Rebellion always leads to judgment. There is much discussion about a local flood, but I believe the obvious intent of Scripture is to make clear that the flood of Noah was a universal flood. I refer to it here because of the crucial nature of the debate:

> *And the flood was forty days upon the earth; and the waters increased, and bare up the ark, and it was lift up above the earth. And the waters prevailed, and were increased greatly upon the*

> *earth; and the ark went upon the face of the waters. And the waters prevailed exceedingly upon the earth; and all the high hills that were under the whole heaven were covered. Fifteen cubits upward did the waters prevail; and the mountains were covered. And all flesh died that moved upon the earth, both of fowl, and of cattle, and of beast, and of every creeping thing that creepeth upon the earth, and every man: All in whose nostrils was the breath of life, of all that was in the dry land, died. And every living substance was destroyed which was upon the face of the ground, both man, and cattle, and the creeping things, and the fowl of the heaven; and they were destroyed from the earth: and Noah only remained alive, and they that were with him in the ark. And the waters prevailed upon the earth an hundred and fifty days* (Genesis 7:17 – 24).

It is nearly impossible to read what God has said and conclude anything other than an all-consuming, all-pervading, universal flood. Notice that Peter (2 Peter 3:4-9) uses the flood as a warning of the judgments that are coming at the end of this age. As man rejected the warnings of God's servant, Noah, so they reject the warnings of God's men today. But every time Noah's hammer rang upon the ark it was crying "judgment is coming" so that they who heard and ignored were without excuse.

REMEDY
The remedy of God is given in Genesis 6:8. God in grace warned Noah, and Noah in faith built the ark to the saving of his household. The ark was the place of safety. Outside were the waters of judgment which overflowed and destroyed "all flesh." The ark is again (as were the coats of skins), a picture of Jesus Christ, who is the "Ark of Salvation."

Those who enter into Christ by faith, do so the same way Noah entered the ark (Hebrews 11:7). Noah committed himself to it in the belief that it could and would save him. Likewise, those who commit themselves to Christ will be saved eternally from the wrath to come (1 Thessalonians 5:9).

Man failed under conscience. He did not lack the inward urge of conscience; perhaps he lacked authority. In the next dispensation we will see how God again added something new. He ordained an authority for man and determined the boundaries for the nations - a new responsibility, a new revelation, and a new test.

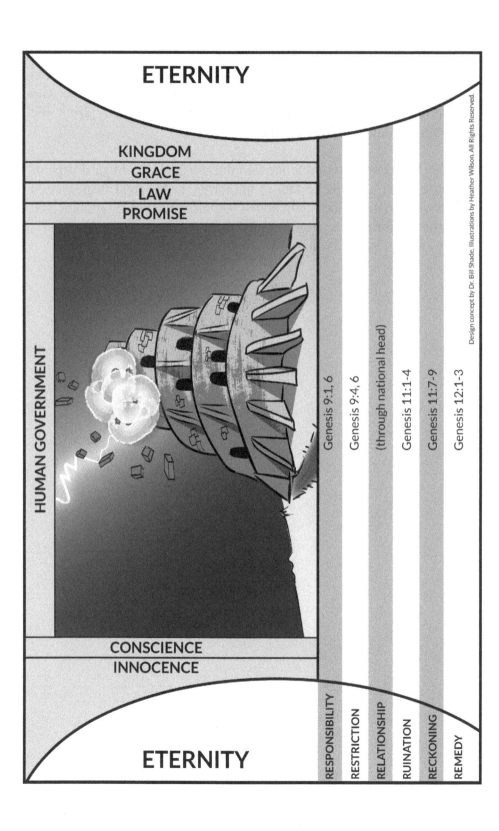

CHAPTER SIX:
THE DISPENSATION OF HUMAN GOVERNMENT

In the preceding chapter we considered how man failed to regulate his actions when left to his conscience. He found that he could (and still can today) rationalize or excuse his way out of feeling guilty for his wrong doings. In this way he silenced his conscience so that it no longer was useful as a regulator of his actions. And since man failed so completely to be governed by his conscience, in what other way might he be guided into righteousness? The question is answered in the Dispensation of Human Government.

While we know from Scripture that God instituted Human Government, we might be tempted to ask, what improvement would such a system have upon the previous Dispensation of Conscience?

It is a well-known trait of human nature that it is easier to judge the faults of others than to see our own. In other words, the ability to discern between right and wrong is always sharper when we are not personally involved. We can easily "see" who is at fault when there is a dispute between others, but when we are involved we quickly develop a moral "blind spot' - we can't see any wrong on our part.

Now since this is true, it seems obvious that if one man or a group of men would undertake to regulate the conduct of other men, the result would be better than simply allowing each man to do, *that which was right in his own eyes* (Judges 21:25). This is the basic principle of Human Government.

In Romans 13:1 we read; *Let every soul be subject unto the higher powers. For there is no power but of God; the powers that be are ordained of God.* In this very plain language, the Holy Spirit thus asserts that Human Government is not the invention of man but the instrument of God. Three times in this passage God refers to Governmental authorities as His *ministers*. As a result God still holds human governments responsible to rule justly and He will hold accountable those He places in positions of authority.

It is also essential to remember that while Human Government failed as a dispensational period of testing, it is still the means God uses to restrain the full outbreak of man's corrupt nature. It has and will continue until, *He (Christ) shall have delivered up the kingdom to God, even the Father, when He shall have put down all rule and all* (human) *authority and power* (1 Corinthians 15:24).

In a recent article on the subject of *Government* Robert Knight observed, "Government is necessary because men are not angels. Its legitimate role is to secure justice by punishing evildoers, and to protect property and individual rights." [1]

It would be well to reflect therefore, that the proper role of Government is not to regulate every action, meet every need, or erase the consequences of foolish actions on the part of its subjects. When Government attempts to relieve us of all difficulties from the cradle to the grave, it has far overstepped its proper role and is one short step from tyranny.

Government's intended function was to punish wrong doing and protect its people, which of necessity would mean establishing and defending its borders. Beyond those functions, Human Government has no biblical mandate.

Let me invite you to look at the chart frequently as we analyze this dispensation.

RESPONSIBILITY

The new dispensation begins after the flood in Genesis 9. It is here that God sets forth man's new responsibilities. First notice the simple command to *be fruitful and replenish the earth* (Genesis 9:1). The Hebrew word translated "replenish" (*maw-lay', maw-law'*) literally means "to fill." Hence, God's first command was to multiply and spread abroad so as to populate the whole earth.

The second command involves the most sacred of all responsibilities; the right and duty to avenge human life. This is commonly called "capital punishment" and is set forth in Genesis 9:5, 6. Notice God says in verse five, *I will require* (i.e. man's blood), and in verse six, *whoso sheddeth man's blood, by man shall his blood be shed.*

The inference then is plain. God requires the blood of any other human being at a murderer's hand. But since God (in verse six) delegates capital punishment to man (*by man shall his blood be shed*), He has placed man in the position of ruling for God.

And herein lays the real test of this dispensation - to see whether man will rule for the glory of God or pervert his prerogative to selfish and sinful ends. It does not take long for the verdict to be in as we shall see in the next two chapters (Genesis 10, 11).

Capital punishment is both the foundation and the capstone of all human government. Where men can avenge murder by taking life, they have entered into the supreme right of any government.

That is why this period is called the Dispensation of Human Government. It is at this point in man's history that God required man to make judgments against wrong doers, and government in all its complexities was the gradual and inevitable outcome.

Notice, I said inevitable, but how so? The full development of government was inevitable because it soon became evident that such a serious matter as executing justice could not be left to the whims and passions of anyone who chose to become a law unto himself. Man learned that he must appoint a "judge" or ruler and that there must be those who would carry out his decisions and protect his sovereignty. So Human Government in all its many layers became a foregone conclusion flowing naturally from its supreme right - the avenging of murder by capital punishment.

How simple and yet how wise are the ways of God. He does not need to set forth a detailed program for government to attain His end. He knows the capstone of all authority is the right to judicially take life, and by simply establishing that, produces the multilayered forms of Human Government to rule for Him. It should be noted also that when this basic function is no longer exercised, governmental authority begins to crumble

Finally, notice that God refers back to the dignity bestowed upon the race at creation as the criterion for government's attitude in dealing with man. *In the image of God created he man.* The fact that man did not retain this image in its first perfection does not lessen the dignity of his original state as created, and it is in the light of that dignity that man must rule for God.

RESTRICTION
The restrictions under the third dispensation are again a reminder that life is from God. The habitation of this mysterious thing called life is stated: The life is in the blood (Genesis 9:4). If human life blood is sacred and not to be shed, then animal life blood is to be held in reverence and not to be eaten – although, notice that at this time God gives His sanction to the eating of animal flesh. The same restrictions (1) against the taking of human life (the shedding of blood) and (2) against the eating of animal blood are later included in the Mosaic Law.

RELATIONSHIP

You will note that under relationship on the chart no reference is given. This is because the relationship must be gleaned from the general tenor of the Scripture and from such histories as *Josephus' Antiquities*. The general practice among the nations from this time on was for the national head (chief or king) to preside as the mediator with God for his people. An Old Testament illustration is Melchizedek (Genesis 14:18). Secular history records the same pattern, which led in some instances to the "deification" of the national head (as per Nimrod, the Pharaohs, Caesars and others).

RUINATION

The ruination of man is set forth in Genesis chapters 10 and 11. In two short chapters we have the sordid tale of man's rebellion and self-deification.

Within six verses of chapter ten we read of *nations* for the first time. Within two more verses we read of the arch-rebel Nimrod who is said to be, *A mighty hunter before the LORD* (Genesis 10:9). The decisive word here is *before* (פנים paw-neem'). Its primary meaning is "against, as in battle." So what we are told is that Nimrod was a mighty hunter (or literally "catcher") against Jehovah. In other words, he was carrying on a war against God.

As we read further in chapter ten and eleven, it becomes abundantly obvious that men were not in any sense "ruling for God," but rather in every sense building their own kingdoms as they have done ever since.

And further, when men began to multiply, God gave orders as to the division of the nations (Genesis 10:5, 20, 25, 32). A close reading will suggest that these instructions were given to Eber (Genesis 10:25) who commemorates them by the naming of his son, Peleg; the literal meaning of which implies "division."

Scripture itself bears testimony to these Divine instructions and God's involvement in the distribution of the nations. Deuteronomy 32:8 reads, *When the most High divided to the nations their inheritance, when he separated the sons of Adam, he set the bounds of the people according to the number of the children of Israel.* God had a plan of His own for the division of the earth among the families of men; and it was probably at this crisis that in some way or other He gave intimation of that plan to the dispersing emigrants through Eber.

Additional evidence of this is found in Paul's words in Acts 17, where we read; *God (that) made the world and all things therein, seeing that he is Lord of heaven and earth, dwelleth not in temples made with hands; Neither is worshipped with men's hands, as though he needed any thing, seeing he giveth to all life, and breath, and all things; And hath made of one blood all nations of men for to dwell on all the face of the earth, and hath determined the times before appointed, and the bounds of their habitation; That they should seek the Lord, if haply they might feel after him, and find him, though he be not far from every one of us: For in him we live, and move, and have our being* (Acts 17:24 - 28). Scripture shows that God has certainly made His purpose clear to man, as regards national distinctions and habitations.

The subsequent judgment reflects the same; for why should God judge man for building a tower and a city unless that building were in direct disobedience to His revealed will? It seems quite obvious that man rebelled against God's direct orders, which we believe were given about mid-way through the dispensation, and under the leadership of Nimrod began to build a world government, *lest we be scattered abroad* (as God had directed) *upon the face of the whole earth* (Genesis 11:4).

Candlish, in his commentary on Genesis writes, "Nimrod and his apostates drew the world after them in an act of daring rebellion against the Most High; and in particular, against His prerogative of dividing to the nations their inheritance; being avowedly intended for the very purpose of preventing the orderly dispersion which God had manifestly appointed." [2]

A further observation may be made of the "Tower Project." Not only was its purpose to unite all men, but the idea of "reaching to heaven," suggests the tower had a profound spiritual dimension as well.

Some have suggested that men were attempting to get to heaven via this tower (*whose top shall reach to heaven*), and others that men were attempting to avert another flood disaster by building such a tower. Such views seem to me a bit naive. If men wanted to escape a flood, why not build a boat? After all, the Ark worked well the first time. Why a tower on a flat plain?

No, the answer seems to be in this; the tower was to be the universal center of a world government and as Alexander Hislop demonstrates in his book, *The Two Babylon's,* the center of a universal religion as well, all in direct rebellion against God's revealed plan for government and religion. [3]

RECKONING
In God's reckoning, notice that the judgment was perfect and appropriate to the sin – *The LORD is known by the judgment which he executeth* (Psalm 9:16). God revealed His plan to divide the people by nations - they refused and rebelled - so God divided them by tongues.

We may be assured that the lines of division outlined by God originally were perfectly followed in this judgment, and so God's purpose was accomplished, but man missed the blessing of obedience. He showed that he could not rule either himself (Proverbs 16:32), or others, and so the dispensation ended in another failure for man.

A word is appropriate here about the origin of language. While humanistic researchers reject the Tower of Babel story as the explanation of the vast variety of human language, every attempt they have made to provide an alternative explanation has failed to satisfy even their own language experts. After a long discussion with a variety of possibilities offered, one writer concludes: "Nevertheless, if we are ever going to learn more about how the human language ability evolved, the most promising evidence will probably come from the human genome, which preserves so much of our species' history. The challenge for the future will be to decode it." 4   The evident fact is that after all the research, they have no answer. The Bible gives the only satisfying answer to the origins and variety of language.

REMEDY
By now you can see clearly the pattern – man is given a revealed Responsibility, certain Restrictions, and a Relationship with God appropriate to his new status. He fails, resulting in Ruination and God then Reckons with him in judgment. But God in each dispensation extends mercy and comes to man with a Remedy.

In this case, God intervened in providing a remedy by choosing a single nation, through which he intends to bring about His grand purposes, not only with that nation itself, but ultimately with the entire human race.

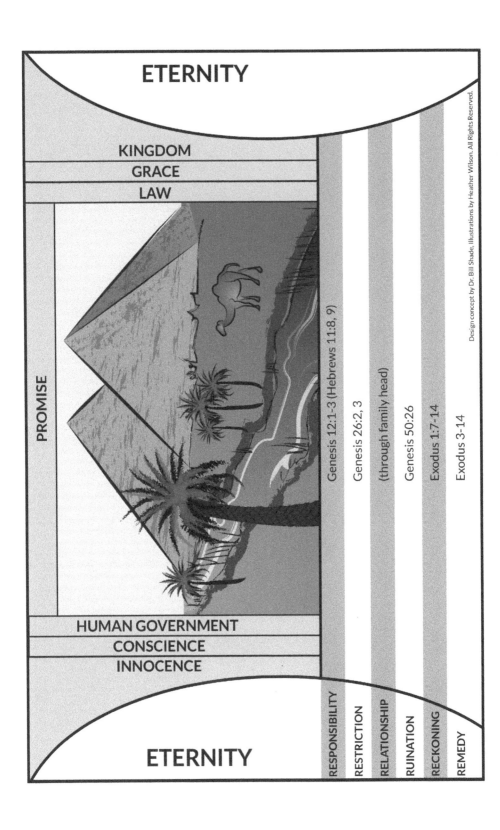

CHAPTER SEVEN:
THE DISPENSATION OF PROMISE

This new dispensation begins with the text of Genesis twelve and the call of Abraham. It is significant that, from the standpoint of time, we have now traveled nearly two thousand years from the Creation. In terms of what we understand as the biblical chronology, we are about one third along the way, and although the amount of recorded history may seem quite small, it has carried us through three major dispensational periods, (i.e., the Dispensations of Innocence, Conscience, and Human Government).

This next dispensation is different in that it does not involve the entire race of humanity, as all the former dispensations did, but is confined to a particular people who will, for the next one third of recorded time, become the focus of God's attention and activity.

Dr. C. I. Scofield makes the following observation,
> "Genesis 11 and 12 mark an important turning point in the divine dealing. Heretofore the history has been that of the whole Adamic race. There has been neither Jew nor Gentile; all have been one in 'the first man Adam.' Henceforth in the Scripture record, humanity must be thought

of as a vast stream from which God, in the call of Abram and the creation of the nation Israel, has but drawn off a slender rill, through which He may (in Christ) purify the great river itself." 1

Dr. Scofield's observation is insightful and his illustration helpful. Seeing that the great river of mankind had utterly polluted itself, God now draws off that slender rill through which He will one day purify the great stream itself. This "rill," of course, is Israel, and it is through Israel that the Redeemer came to provide purification for all men (1 John 2:2).

It cannot be stressed too frequently that from Genesis 12 to Acts 10 God is dealing primarily with Israel. The Old Testament is written almost entirely by the Jew, about the Jew, and to the Jew. If you get this firmly in mind so that you recognize and account for it in all you read and study, you have gotten one of the "Master Keys" to an understanding of the Scriptures.

In Genesis chapter twelve, God began this new work of dealing with a single nation (instead of all mankind) by calling a single man out of heathen idolatry to walk with Him. This man was Abram (Abraham). Notice that God had promised to *dwell in the tents of Shem* (Genesis 9:27), and in keeping with this promise, He chose a Shemite for this new work.

God's call of Abraham was purely of grace, *that the purpose of God according to election might stand, not of works, but of him that calleth;). . . So then it is not of him that willeth, nor of him that runneth,* (i.e. works for the blessing) *but of God that sheweth mercy* (Romans 9:11-16). Along with God's gracious call there were given to Abraham certain PROMISES, from which this new dispensation takes its name.

After Abraham's initial step of faith in leaving Ur and going into the land of Canaan, these promises became unconditional; that is, they depended upon God alone for their fulfillment. However, in order to receive the full blessing of God's promises, Abraham had to dwell in the land.

We see then that though the promises were dependent only upon the faithfulness of God, the blessing of enjoying those promises depended upon Abraham's obedience. He, and his descendents, must stay in the land (Genesis 26:2, 3). Often Abraham's faith faltered and finally his posterity failed completely and the period of testing ended *in a coffin in Egypt* (Genesis 50:26).

God's purpose in the call of Abraham may be seen in the following verses:

- They were to be Jehovah witnesses. (Isaiah 43:10). Note: The Russelite's use of this phrase as a name for their devilish cult is an illustration of what happens when we fail to *rightly divide the word of truth*. The title was given to the nation Israel, not a conglomerate Gentile cult!

- Israel was to receive and preserve for the world the divine revelation - God's Word (Romans 3:1, 2).

- Israel was to bring forth from among themselves the Redeemer of the World (Romans 9:4, 5; Matthew 1:1).

Analyzing the Dispensation of Promise (Please refer to the chart)

RESPONSIBILITY
The feature which best characterizes this dispensation is that it is a period of "Promise." Not just a single promise, but rather a whole host of promises given to Abraham and to his posterity and confirmed by covenant. In Genesis twelve the Abrahamic Covenant is briefly outlined, then reaffirmed and defined in chapter thirteen, ratified by sacrifice in chapter fifteen, sealed by the sign of circumcision in chapter

seventeen, and eternally secured by the oath of God Himself in chapter twenty two.

We recognize within that covenant the promises of:

(1) **The Land** (defined as; *from the river of Egypt unto the great river, the river Euphrates* – Genesis 15:18).

(2) **A Seed,** which included a posterity comparable to the sand of the seashore and the stars of heaven, but which specifically included, as we learn from the New Testament (Galatians 3:16), that Seed through which the nations of the world would be blessed, that is Christ.

(3) **A Blessing,** *I will bless him that blesseth thee and curse him that curseth thee,* and again the promise that God would bless the entire race through Abraham.

These then were the promises that become the focus of this dispensation.

These covenant promises were then passed on to Abraham's posterity; first to Isaac (Genesis 26:2–5) and later to Jacob (Genesis 28:12–15). Dwelling on these great promises the Psalmist said:

> *He hath remembered his covenant for ever, the word which he commanded to a thousand generations. Which covenant he made with Abraham, and his oath unto Isaac; And confirmed the same unto Jacob for a law, and to Israel for an everlasting covenant: Saying, Unto thee will I give the land of Canaan, the lot of your inheritance: When they were but a few men in number; yea, very few, and strangers in it* (Psalm 105:8 – 12).

In fact, it would be well to read and meditate upon the entire Psalm because it is all about believing God's promises and acting upon them, even when circumstances seem to contradict what God has said. And that is the great test of the Dispensation of Promise.

We pay great respect to a man when we take him at his word. And we please God when we believe what He has spoken and act upon the conviction that His promises are faithful and true. It requires faith to believe, and so God calls forth faith in the Dispensation of Promise.

RESTRICTION
In harmony with Abraham's Responsibility was the Restriction laid upon him (see the chart) that he should *dwell in the Land*. If he believed the promise of God that he would be blessed, he would stay in the land, regardless of what the immediate circumstances seemed to be.

When Abraham and his posterity went out of the land (Genesis 12:10-20; 20:1-18; 26:1-35; 28:10-15), they were manifesting their unbelief in the promises of God. In each instance, the one who left the land met with trouble, and although God prospered each one, they usually returned having reason to wish that they had never left. We derive the greatest happiness through walking in obedience to God.

When in the course of His Sovereign will, God actually took them out of the Land to preserve them for a time in Egypt (and to make of them there a great nation), those who were faithful to the promises never lost sight of the Land. Jacob required that they carry him back to the Land and bury him there (Genesis 49:29 – 33). When Joseph died he requested the same (Genesis 50:24, 25), and it is significant that it is this act of faith for which he is remembered by God in the words, *By faith Joseph, when he died, made mention of the departing of the children of Israel; and gave commandment concerning his bones* (Hebrews 11:22).

So, even when God made provision for them in Egypt they were not to forget His promises and the Land which God had promised to them.

RELATIONSHIP

As in the former dispensation, there is no direct verse which sets forth man's relationship with God. A reading of the Scripture this period covers, however, will show that God dealt with His people through the family (or tribal) head – the Patriarch. In Abraham's family it was the one who had, by inheritance, received the promises and become heir to the covenant made with Abraham. The Patriarchs were Abraham, Isaac, and Jacob.

RUINATION

While God placed Israel in Egypt and blessed them, the blessings were never meant to cloud out the promises of God, but this is, it appears, exactly what happened.

Joseph had placed them in the area of Goshen, one of the most fruitful places in Egypt. God's description of their situation is recorded in these words:

> *And the children of Israel were fruitful, and increased abundantly, and multiplied, and waxed exceeding mighty; and the land was filled with them* (Exodus 1:7).

One commentator says of them, "Thus in about two hundred and fifteen years they were multiplied to upwards of 600,000, independently of old men, women, and children." [2]

However, the prosperity they enjoyed was accompanied by a loss of interest in the promises of God and ultimately a loss of even an awareness of them. It is not without significance that the book of Genesis which begins with the sublime words, *In the beginning God created the heaven and the earth*, ends with the words, *in a coffin in Egypt*.

Indeed, those words seem to describe their eventual spiritual condition as settled down in the prosperity of Egypt. Israel's prosperity in Egypt made them forget the promises of God and the Promised Land. They were satisfied to remain in Egypt, and the hopes of a better country became dim and at last faded away.

RECKONING

God always answers our failures with chastening, and though *no chastening for the present seemeth to be joyous but grievous, nevertheless afterward it yieldeth the peaceable fruit of righteousness to them which are exercised thereby* (Hebrews 12:11). God allowed things to become grievous for Israel so that they would once again lift their eyes to the promise and long for a better land.

The Scripture records it in these words,

> *Now there arose up a new king over Egypt, which knew not Joseph. And he said unto his people, Behold, the people of the children of Israel are more and mightier than we: Come on, let us deal wisely with them; lest they multiply, and it come to pass, that, when there falleth out any war, they join also unto our enemies, and fight against us, and so get them up out of the land. Therefore they did set over them taskmasters to afflict them with their burdens. And they built for Pharaoh treasure cities, Pithom and Raamses. But the more they afflicted them, the more they multiplied and grew. And they were grieved because of the children of Israel. And the Egyptians made the children of Israel to serve with rigour: And they made their lives bitter with hard bondage, in morter, and in brick, and in all manner of service in the field: all their service, wherein they made them serve, was with rigour* (Exodus 1:8 – 14).

REMEDY

The remedy came with the commissioning of Moses to *bring forth my people the children of Israel out of Egypt* (Exodus 3:10). Through Moses, God judged the nation of Egypt and proved their gods to be worthless (Numbers 33:4). With a mighty hand, Jehovah delivered His people.

They did not deserve God's mercy, but God dealt with them in grace until they presumptuously adjudged themselves able to keep a perfect law and entered upon a conditional covenant that opens a new dispensation and carries us all the way through the Old Testament into the New.

One thing that dispensational studies teach us is that while all of the Bible is **for us** - not all of the Bible is written **to us**. Much of it was written to the Jews, the primary people of the Old Testament. If we apply this principle in regard to the promises of God, we will not make the foolish mistake of claiming for ourselves some of the earthly promises made only to Israel in the Old Testament.

That is the error made by many of the popular movements of our time (i.e., the Wealth and Prosperity Gospel; the Kingdom Now, etc.). The promises made to us in this Dispensation of Grace are primarily heavenly (John 16:33; Ephesians 1:3). But remember this, every promise made **to us** is sure, and we should claim each as our very own by faith (2 Corinthians 1:20).

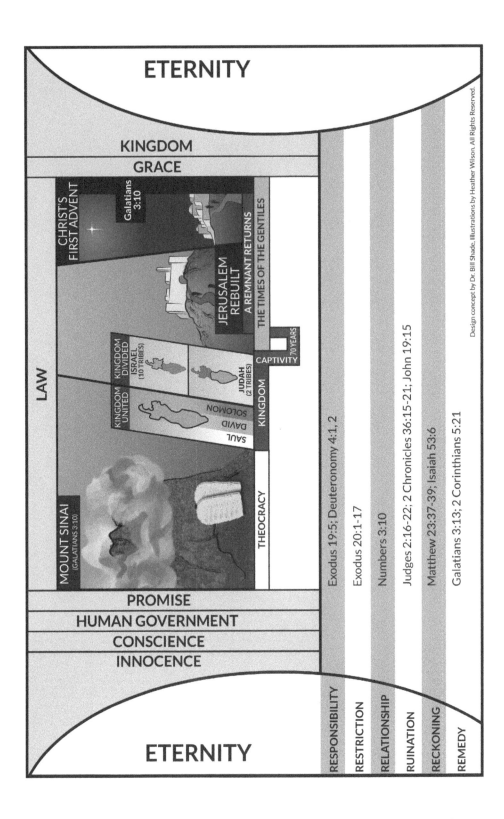

CHAPTER EIGHT:
THE DISPENSATION OF LAW
-The Law Given

The beginning of the Dispensation of Law brings us to the 19th chapter of the book of Exodus where God prepares His people for this new dispensation. The Apostle Paul explains this change like this: *Wherefore then serveth the law? It was added because of transgressions, till the seed should come to whom the promise was made; and it was ordained by angels in the hand of a mediator* (Galatians 3:19). The question left unanswered by the preceding verse is "to what was the Law added?"

Up until this point God has dealt with Israel in pure grace. There was nothing, from a natural point of view, which caused God to deliver Israel from bondage. It was not that they were better or bigger or more righteous than any other people. It is just that God, in sovereign grace, and in respect to His covenants with the Patriarchs, loved them and chose to deliver them and redeem them.

You will *notice* that God accomplished everything – Israel, nothing! When Pharaoh refused to release them, God delivered them by the plagues until the Egyptians literally *drove them out*. When they stood helpless by the sea, God opened the sea and destroyed their enemies. When they would have perished for hunger in the wilderness, God gave them manna from heaven. When they fainted for thirst in the desert, God gave them water from the flinty rock.

What was their attitude all this while? They accused Moses the servant of God (Exodus 14:11,12), they murmured and complained (Exodus 15:24; 16:2, 7), and they tempted God by their persistent demands and unreasonable unbelief (Exodus 17:2).

Please observe that God's dealing with Israel was pure grace (undeserved favor and blessing) because (1) God loved them (*for God is love*) and (2) because God remembered His promises to Abraham made so many centuries before.

So the answer to the question is this; "the Law was added to the **grace** God had so abundantly bestowed." Consider Moses' words:

> *The LORD did not set his love upon you, nor choose you, because ye were more in number than any people; for ye were the fewest of all people: But because the LORD loved you, and because he would keep the oath which he had sworn unto your fathers, hath the LORD brought you out with a mighty hand, and redeemed you out of the house of bondmen, from the hand of Pharaoh king of Egypt* (Deuteronomy 7:7, 8).

While there is a specific sense in which the dispensation since Calvary has been called the Dispensation of Grace, the former dispensations were not without the grace of God. Had that been the case, man would have quickly perished from the earth.

Something took place in Exodus 19 however, which changed God's method of dealing with Israel and brought in a new dispensation. After all of God's blessings in grace, God tested Israel by offering to them a covenant relationship which would condition God's future blessings to Israel on their implicit obedience to God's law.

Rather than considering their continued failures and falling in humility before God, acknowledging their absolute inability to fulfill the perfect obedience required by a conditional covenant (the law), they proudly and haughtily replied, *All that the LORD hath spoken we will do* (Exodus 19:8). Thus began the Dispensation of Law. Henceforth, God must deal with them in justice and require complete obedience. To fall short, or to overstep (disobey) the Law, meant that the penalty for a broken Law must be paid in full.

Analyzing the Dispensation of Law (Please look at the section of theChart provided in the beginning of this chapter)

RESPONSIBILITY
Read carefully Exodus 19:5. Notice the condition stated in the words, *if ye will*. Also notice the words, *then ye shall be.* Now we have the Key to God's dealings with Israel under Law. Israel would become *a peculiar treasure...a kingdom of priests, and an holy nation,* **IF** they would keep the Law in its entirety.

Just how exacting the requirements of keeping the Law really are may be seen by reading Deuteronomy 4:1, 2.

> *Now therefore hearken, O Israel, unto the statutes and unto the judgments, which I teach you, for to do them, that ye may live, and go in and possess the land which the LORD God of your fathers giveth you. Ye shall not add unto the word which I command you, neither shall ye diminish ought from it, that ye may keep the commandments of the LORD your God which I command you.*

Ye shall not add...neither shall ye diminish ought from it. That is perfect, absolute, and complete adherence to all points, at all times. And that is exactly what the Law demands! It is what James tells us in his Epistle:

> *For whosoever shall keep the whole law, and yet offend in one point, he is guilty of all* (James 2:10).

Or consider Paul's words in his Epistle to the Galatians:

> *For as many as are of the works of the law are under the curse: for it is written, Cursed is every one that continueth not in all things which are written in the book of the law to do them* (Galatians 3:10).

It is all-important that we understand the true nature of the Law or we will never understand this dispensation or the next.

There are many people who feel (and some religious sects which teach) that these requirements are not as rigid as they appear on the surface. They argue that it would be impossible for man to keep the Law if it were absolute. God, they say, would not ask man to do what was impossible for him. Obedience to these commands and their demands is relative.

The Law, however, is not relative but absolute – as Isaiah says, *To the law and to the testimony: if they speak not according to this word, it is because there is no light in them* (Isaiah 8:20).

No, the fact is that the Law is impossible for man to keep because in its essence, the Law is a reflection of the righteousness of God. It therefore requires that we be as good as God – and this we cannot do. But Israel and all men had to learn this and be made to face their own weakness and depravity.

So God accepted their proud declaration (Exodus 19:8), and placed them under the Dispensation of Law with the responsibility to fulfill perfectly a perfect law, and, hence, "be as good as God."

RESTRICTION

If you are looking at the chart, you will see the reference for that first part of the Law, the Decalogue or Ten Commandments. This is, however, not all of the law, and it is important to remember that the whole Law was the responsibility of the man under Law.

Exodus 21 to 23 inclusive, records the social law or judgments, and Exodus 24 to 31 inclusive, sets forth the religious or ceremonial law. Each had its necessary function, and each was binding on all of the nation.

The moral law, or Ten Commandments, expressed God's nature and will, particularly as concerns (a) man's relationship to God (commandments 1-4), and (b) man's relationship to others (commandments 5-10).

The judgments are mainly an enlargement of commandments 5 - 10; that is, man's relationship to others. I have sometimes compared them to the flight rules I had to observe as a pilot. The rules themselves were published in one book, and accompanying that was a second book entitled, "Accepted Methods of Complying with FAA Regulations".

The "judgments" may be thought of in one respect as accepted methods of complying with commandments 5-10." However, we must realize that they are also an enlargement and extension of the commandments, attaching certain penalties to those who would disobey.

The ceremonial law was related to the first four commandments in somewhat the same manner as the judgments were related to the last six. It taught *that the way into the holiest of all* (the very presence of God) was shut off because of sin; that the *wages of sin is death*, and that *without shedding of blood* there could be no taking away of sins. All this carried tremendous typical significance, pointing ahead to *the Lamb of God, which taketh away the sin of the world* (John 1:29).

RELATIONSHIP
Through sin, Israel failed of the high goal of becoming a "kingdom of priests," and the priesthood was shut up to the tribe of Levi and the family of Aaron. Notice the verse given on the chart: *And thou shalt appoint Aaron and his sons, and they shall wait on the priest's office: and the stranger that cometh nigh shall be put to death* (Numbers 3:10).

It was Aaron's job to minister the ceremonies and sacrifices of the tabernacle. The tabernacle was erected to deal with the anticipated matter of a broken law. No tabernacle would have meant no atonement (the covering made for sin by shedding blood), and no atonement would have meant no way for God to deal with them in mercy. God would have been forced by the very holiness of His own nature and the demands of a broken law to destroy Israel *entirely* for their sin. But God's mercy entered in and provided a way to escape.

God instituted the tabernacle sacrifices to cover the sins under the old covenant (the Law) until His Son should take them away by the sacrifice of Himself (Romans 3:25; Hebrews 9:15). The function of the priesthood was to implement the tabernacle services and to serve in the shadows of heavenly things until our Great High Priest would take up His heavenly ministrations. The Priests were, for Israel, the only approach to God, and so the link of Relationship in the Dispensation of Law.

While God could no longer deal with Israel in pure grace since they were under the Law, He did deal with them in mercy through the tabernacle offerings. This fact brings out a precious and often neglected differentiation between these two attributes of God.

Grace gives man what he does not deserve (i.e., salvation, forgiveness, eternal life, and an inheritance incorruptible and eternal). Mercy withholds from man what he does deserve (i.e., God's righteous judgment against sin; 2 Peter 3:9). The Tabernacle sacrifices allowed God to "cover" a broken Law, until its full penalty would be satisfied by a Perfect Substitute.

CHAPTER NINE:
THE DISPENSATION OF LAW
-Three Periods Under Law

After receiving the Law at Sinai, Israel as a nation lived under the Dispensation of Law for approximately 1,500 years. During this time, there were three distinct periods through which the nation passed.

If you are familiar with the history of Israel, you might at first dispute that statement. History appears to teach that Israel lived through at least five periods: the wilderness wanderings, the period of the judges, the period of the kings, the exile, and the period of the restoration.

However, when we study Israel's relation to the Law more closely, we find that a central part of the Law had to do with the Land itself. The Law and the land of Palestine, Israel's "Promised Land" went together.

In fact, there were portions of the Law that could not be kept until and unless Israel was in the Land. God had commanded that three times a year Israel's men were to gather, *in the place which He shall choose* (Deuteronomy 16:16). It could never be observed during those periods when Israel was exiled from the Land. The *Place* also involved the sacrifices.

They were not to be offered except in the *Place* of God's choosing (Leviticus 17).

The Feasts of Jehovah were intricately tied to the Land. The Feast of Passover, at the beginning of the year was only observed one time during the forty years of wandering in the wilderness, but was the first Feast to be commemorated upon reaching the Land (Joshua 5:10).

The Feast of Firstfruits, was obviously impossible to keep apart from the Land. There would be no Firstfruits (or any other fruits), either in the wilderness or in captivity. The same would be true of most of the other Feasts. These were a part of the Law, but impossible to observe outside the Land.

Laws concerning the Sabbath were a problem. Israel could keep the weekly Sabbaths in the wilderness or in the Land, but in captivity even that was often taken from her by the demands of her captors.

And the weekly Sabbath was only a part of the Law. The Law demanded a seventh year Sabbath, and a Sabbath of Sabbaths called the year of Jubilee. None of that was possible outside the Land.

So when we talk about the periods of Israel's history under the Law, we see at once that the Law and the Land were so intertwined that we can only count that time that Israel dwelt in the Land. In the land then, Israel passed through three periods under the Law.

RUINATION (Three strikes and you're out)

The Period of the Theocracy:
Once Israel was established in the land, God began ruling through the judges. Up until then, the great leaders Moses and Joshua had led the people. Now God raised up fourteen judges to lead and to deliver His people during these early days in the land.

There were thirteen men and one woman judge. The first was Othniel, and the last was Samuel. During this time Israel had a theocracy – that is, God was the real King of Israel and was ruling through His judges. When the people demanded a king, God said; . . . *for they have not rejected thee* (Samuel), *but they have rejected me, that I should not reign over them* (1 Samuel 8:7). Here then the theocracy ended.

During this time Israel failed miserably. Read the verses on the chart (Judges 2:16-22). Some of the crimes and confusion of that time have been pointed at by skeptics and unbelievers through the years as examples of the religion of Moses.

Actually, the book of Judges is an example of the lawlessness of a nation under Law. Again and again we read, *In those days there was no king in Israel; every man did that which was right in his own eyes* (Judges 21:25).

Think of it! No king because they had rejected God as their King and become lawless renegades. This was the nation that had said at Sinai, *all that the LORD hath spoken we will do.* The period ended in a prolonged era of about 200 years of silence from God and civil and religious strife among the people.

The Period of the Kingdom:
After Israel received a king, they began to make a new beginning. Under the leadership of Samuel, and then David, the Law was reinstated (it had been in effect all along but was ignored) and the tabernacle service was given a prominent place. Jerusalem was chosen as the place of worship (1 Kings 11:36), and during the reign of Solomon, the great temple was erected.

Not that there was perfect obedience to the moral law, there never could be. But by compliance with the moral law in part and by recourse to the temple sacrifices which atoned for failures (*made a covering for sin* – did not take sin away), the people were happy, prosperous, and enjoyed God's blessing.

The condition, however, did not last, as a reading of the book of Kings will show, and the period ended in complete apostasy.

First, the kingdom divided under Rehoboam, and the Kings of the northern ten tribes never again kept any semblance of God's Law. The history of the southern kingdom of Judah and Benjamin was the story of a long decent downward with intermittent periods of revival, followed by renewed and added apostasy.

The northern kingdom (Israel) only went deeper into sin as time went along until its history ended. Notice that its history ended before the southern kingdom of Judah by about 140 years. This period is covered by the books of Samuel, Kings, and Chronicles. Once again you can read the Divine Commentary on Israel's failure in the verses on the chart (2 Chronicles 36:15-21).

The Period of the Restoration:
After the failure under the period of Kings, Israel went into exile. Here they were somewhat like a man in jail who is supposed to be tending his garden. They were obligated to the Law but not in any practical sense able to perform it. They could not carry out the ceremonial Law or the judgments, and the moral Law only condemned them and left them without recourse. They were, indeed, in a desperate condition. But after seventy years (refer again to the chart), according to the prophecy of Jeremiah, God restored a remnant to the land.

I want to point out several important features here – Israel was cured of idolatry. Seventy years captivity in the very pit of idolatry (Babylon) had immunized her to the disease of idol worship. She was wedded strictly to the Law. She became the great teacher of the Law (Romans 2:17-21). But she missed entirely the real purpose of the Law. Israel became formalistic and hypocritical. She observed the strict teaching of the rabbis and justified herself through external adherence to the Law.

However, when God sent His Son, *made under the Law* (Galatians 4:4), and a living incarnation of all that the Law demanded, they hated Him, rejected Him, and crucified Him. Yet, He was the fulfillment of the Law, for He, alone, was "as good as God"; in fact, He was God.

Christ faced the rich young ruler with this fact. He had acknowledged the goodness of Christ by calling Him *Good Master. Jesus said . . . there is none good but One, that is God;* implying, "If I am not God, I am not good" (Luke 18:19).

The final failure of Israel under Law is exposed in the words of John 19:15:

> *But they cried out, Away with him, away with him, crucify him. Pilate saith unto them, Shall I crucify your King? The chief priests answered, We have no king but Caesar.*

Israel, had been up to the plate three times and in three attempts she had failed. Israel "struck out" as far as her performance under the Law was concerned.

RECKONING:
Listen to the words of our Lord Himself:

> *O Jerusalem, Jerusalem, thou that killest the prophets, and stonest them which are sent unto thee, how often would I have gathered thy children together, even as a hen gathereth her chickens under her wings, and ye would not! Behold, your house is left unto you desolate. For I say unto you, Ye shall not see me henceforth, till ye shall say, Blessed is he that cometh in the name of the Lord* (Matthew 23:37 – 39).

Israel as a nation was desolate – rejected. She is dwelling to this day under the curse of Lo-ammi; *Then said God, ye are not my people and I will not be your God* (Hosea 1:8, 9). Her house is desolate.

She has no sacrifice (Hosea 3:4), no priesthood (Hebrews 7:11, 12), and no hope (Jeremiah 18:12). She is blind (Romans 11:7, 25), hardened (Acts 7:51-53), and accounted an enemy of God and His gospel (Romans 11:28). Yet Israel will not always dwell in *the valley of the shadow of death.* God has a plan for this nation.

REMEDY:
While setting Israel aside nationally for the time being, God nevertheless dealt with them in mercy once again in that He judged their crimes and horrible sinfulness, not upon their own heads, but upon the Head of His own Beloved Son. It is for this reason that Israel shall some day, *look upon Him whom they pierced* and wail for Him (Zechariah 12:10), and be converted to the Savior they once rejected.

Remember the words of Isaiah 53:6, *All we like sheep have gone astray, we have turned every one to his own way, and the LORD hath laid upon Him* (Jesus*) the iniquity of us all.* We often apply this to ourselves and as an application it is perfectly true. God did lay our sins upon Christ, and Christ did bear them away. But in the context, Isaiah 53 indicates that God laid the sins of a nation (i.e., Israel) upon His Son.

That was the same truth which came from the mouth of Caiaphas when he said, *it is expedient for us, that one man should die for the people, and that the whole nation perish not. And this spake he not of himself: but being high priest that year, he prophesied that Jesus should die for that nation* (John 11:50, 51).

God's Remedy for a broken Law and a failed dispensation was to require the penalty at the hand of His Son, *For Christ is the end of the law for righteousness to every one that believeth* (Romans 10:4). The one who seeks to meet God on the basis of the Law instead of coming to Christ to receive salvation and forgiveness as a gift by faith, will be judged by the Law he professes to keep. In this sense then, the Law is still in effect and always will be, but as a dispensational period, the Law ended at Calvary. *Christ is the end of the law* (Romans 10:4).

CHAPTER TEN:
THE DISPENSATION OF LAW
-The Purpose of the Law

The question of the real purpose of the Law, is posed by Bunyan in his immortal classic, Pilgrim's Progress. One of Bunyan's characters, "Evangelist" had instructed "Pilgrim" in the right way, but he had been turned aside by several false teachers whom Bunyan characteristically names Mr. Legality, Mr. Worldly Wiseman and Mr. Civility. These three imposters pointed Pilgrim to the Law in order to be freed from his burden of sin and so Pilgrim was trying to find release from his sins through the Law.

Coming to Mount Sinai, Pilgrim found, not peace and release, but the thunderous roar of the Law's condemnation which could only leave him in despair. Evangelist, finding him rebukes him with these words:

> "This Legality, (the Law), is not able to set thee free from thy burden. No man was as yet ever rid of his burden by him; no, nor ever is like to be: ye cannot be justified by the works of the Law; for by the deeds of the Law no man living can be rid of his burden: Therefore, Mr. Worldly Wiseman is an alien, and Mr. Legality is a cheat; and for his son Civility, notwithstanding his simpering looks, he is

but a hypocrite and cannot help thee. Believe me, there is nothing in all this noise that thou hast heard of these stupid men, but a design to beguile thee of thy salvation, by turning thee from the way in which I had set thee". 1

The sense of Bunyan's words are easily discernible. The Law cannot save and was never intended to do so. What then is the Law and why was it given?

First, the Law was given as a revelation. A revelation is that which makes known what before was dark or hidden. As a revelation, the Law uncovered three things, all of which are found in Romans chapter seven.

The Law revealed what sin is. Paul writes, *I had not known sin but by the law* (Romans 7:7). The Law defined sin and gave it its character. Dr. C.I. Scofield says it well:

> "Sin is transgression, an over-stepping of the divine boundary between good and evil; Iniquity, an act inherently wrong...; Error, a departure from right; Missing the mark, a failure to reach the divine standard; Trespass, the intrusion of self-will into the sphere of divine authority; Lawlessness, or spiritual anarchy; and Unbelief, an insult to the divine veracity (truthfulness) (Psalm 51; Luke 15:29; Romans 3). Law revealed that sin was defiling (Leviticus 18.30) and constituted guilt (Leviticus 4:13, 14). 2

By the Law is the knowledge of sin.

Secondly, the Law revealed what man is. We have already noted how the Ceremonial Law showed man's defilement and forbade him to approach God's holiness because of it. In Romans 7:8, 9, we have an additional revelation. Paul says, *But sin, taking occasion by the commandment, wrought in me all manner of concupiscence.*

In other words, the Law actually aggravated the sinful nature in man. It was like telling a child that he could not have a certain toy. Suddenly it was the only toy in the world he really wanted. So the Law forbade; and man's nature responded by desiring the forbidden. The Law thus revealed a sinful heart.

Finally, the Law revealed the holiness of God. What kind of God was this that brought Israel out of Egypt? Was He like the gods of the other nations - sensual, immoral, greedy, and cruel? The Law was God's answer to this question.

When we read the description of the giving of the Law in Exodus chapters nineteen and twenty, the whole scene is filled with awe and terror. God commanded perfect cleanness, (sanctify yourselves) and absolute obedience. *Wherefore the law is holy and the commandment holy, and just and good* (Romans 7:12). Thus the Law revealed sin, man, and God.

However, the Law is not only a revelation; it is an **obligation**. James says that a man who looks into the perfect Law and does nothing about it is like the person who, looking in a mirror, discovers that he has a dirty face, and then turns away and leaves it just as dirty as before. The Law was never intended simply for information, but for obedience, and that obedience had to be perfect. If someone failed at any point for one moment, he came under condemnation (James 2:10).

Not only does the Law demand perfect obedience, but it curses and condemns disobedience. The Law knows no mercy. It is justice - pure and unremitting:

> *And while the children of Israel were in the wilderness, they found a man that gathered sticks upon the sabbath day. And they that found him gathering sticks brought him unto Moses and Aaron, and unto all the congregation. And they put him in ward, because it was not declared what should be done to him. And the LORD said unto*

> *Moses, The man shall be surely put to death: all the congregation shall stone him with stones without the camp. And all the congregation brought him without the camp, and stoned him with stones, and he died; as the LORD commanded Moses* (Numbers 15:32-36).
>
> *He that despised Moses' law died without mercy under two or three witnesses* (Hebrews 10:28).

Since the Law demands nothing short of perfection, and all have sinned and disobeyed the Law (Romans 3:23; Acts 7:53) all are therefore under its curse (Galatians 3:10). It strips man of all pretension to self-righteousness and exposes him before God utterly condemned and so guilty that he is without excuse and speechless (Romans 3:19).

Finally, the Law shuts man up to faith as the only possible way of escape (Galatians 3:23). God meant that man should find no comfort in the Law – after all, how could he? It revealed God's holiness and man's sinfulness and cursed the latter that it might glorify the former. The Law offered absolutely no hope – *for by the works of the law shall no flesh be justified* (Galatians 2.16).

Now, it is evident that if Law works could not set man right with God, no works could avail. There was only one recourse; man could look to God for mercy, and trust Him to provide a way of forgiveness by faith. God intended the Law to lead Israel to Christ as their only hope for salvation (Galatians 3:24). Instead, they justified themselves in their own sight by an external fulfillment of the Law, without any heart change, and failed of the righteousness required.

> *But Israel, which followed after the law of righteousness, hath not attained to the law of righteousness. Wherefore? Because they sought it not by faith, but as it were by the works of the law. For they stumbled at that stumblingstone; As it is*

> *written, Behold, I lay in Sion a stumblingstone and rock of offence: and whosoever believeth on him shall not be ashamed* (Romans 9.31-33).

Paul continues on the same theme in the next chapter:

> *Brethren, my heart's desire and prayer to God for Israel is, that they might be saved. For I bear them record that they have a zeal of God, but not according to knowledge. For they being ignorant of God's righteousness, and going about to establish their own righteousness, have not submitted themselves unto the righteousness of God. For Christ is the end of the law for righteousness to every one that believeth* (Romans 10:1 - 4).

They, therefore, remained under the curse, for *cursed is everyone that continueth not in all things which are written in the book of the law, to do them* (Galatians 3:10).

But what was Christ's relationship to the Law? In the first place Christ was *made of a woman, made under the law* (Galatians 4:4). By His perfect life He answered all of the demands of the Law for righteousness. He would say of Himself, *Think not that I am come to destroy the law, or the prophets: I am not come to destroy, but to fulfill* (Matthew 5:17).

Christ fulfilled the Law and the prophets, by exceeding all the demands for righteousness the Law made, and then by providing the perfect sacrifice which the Law demanded and which the prophets had foretold. If what the prophets predicted and the Law demanded were fulfilled, then the work of the Law was complete.

Even His severest critics could find no fault in Him (John 8:46; 18:23, 38). He alone could say, *I do always those things which please Him* [the Father] (John 8:29). Even Judas, the betrayer, confessed, *I betrayed the innocent blood* (Matthew 27:4). And one of His closest associates testified that He *did no sin* (1 Peter 2:22). Paul testified that He *knew no sin* (2 Corinthians 5:21), and being virgin born of God, He had no sin. Every demand of being "as good as God" which the Law made, Christ met.

Now, how does all of that relate to us? Such holiness only condemned us the more. Here was a man *tempted in all points like as we are*, yet never sinning. Christ's holy life accomplished nothing so far as our salvation is concerned, except that it proved Him the conqueror of the Law. He was the perfect veil that had to be rent to allow us access to God.

Then the Holy, Spotless One made the supreme sacrifice. He who knew no sin, and to whose account the Law could lay not one single charge, took all of the guilt of all the world and *became sin for us* (2 Corinthians 5:21). When he did, the very Law He had fulfilled condemned Him with its curse, and *He became a curse for us* (Galatians 3:13).

God thus vindicated the claims of the Law by slaying the One who stood up to meet its terrible justice. All the arrows of God's wrath against sin sunk into the heart of the Savior, and He met every claim the Law had against us by paying its penalty in full. And when He was rent at the Cross, the symbolic veil was rent as well, and the way opened for every believing sinner to come to God.

The Dispensation of Law ended when, *Christ delivered us from the curse of the law, being made a curse for us, for it is written, cursed is everyone that hangeth on a tree* (Galatians 3:13). By paying our debt to a broken Law in full, He made salvation available to us as a gift to be received simply by faith in Him.

The result is stated clearly in Acts 13:39; *And by him* (Christ) *all that believe are justified from all things, from which ye could not be justified by the law of Moses.*

Notice that we have tried to indicate this truth on the left arm of the cross found on the chart. Law ended when "Jesus paid it all." *The wages of sin (demanded by the Law) is death, but the gift of God is eternal life through Jesus Christ our Lord* (Romans 6:23). There is nothing left now but Grace, and that brings us to the sixth and present dispensation – The Dispensation of Grace.

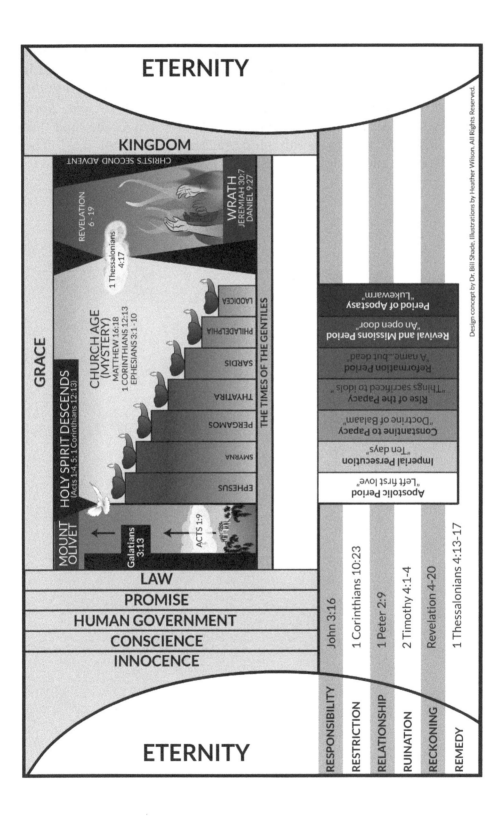

CHAPTER ELEVEN:
THE DISPENSATION OF GRACE
-Some Vital Explanations

In order to properly understand this dispensation, I want to encourage you to begin by looking carefully at the section of the chart which covers this period. Much of what we want to cover can be best understood by becoming very familiar with that part of the chart.

You will find this dispensation between the "Cross" (which marks the beginning of the dispensation), and the descending arrow which is labeled "Christ's Second Advent," which marks its end. These are located above the double horizontal lines in the center of the chart which indicate TIME by running from "eternity past" to "eternity future."

The second thing we must do in approaching this dispensation is to distinguish the dispensation itself from the primary program God is carrying out during this dispensation. While the two things are contemporaneous, they are not identical. During this Dispensation of Grace, which extends from the Cross to the Second Coming, Christ is building His Church.

Jesus declared, *I will build my church; and the gates of hell shall not prevail against it* (Matthew 16:18). Note our Lord's use of the future tense - *I will*. This indicates the Church was not being built during our Lord's earthly ministry, but was to be built in the future.

The New Testament Church, which is the Body of Christ was planned of God to be begun and completed during this Dispensation of Grace, but the Church Age (the period when the Church is being built), and the Dispensation of Grace are distinct.

In carrying out His program, Christ gave birth to His mystical Body, the Church, at Pentecost through the baptism of the Holy Spirit (Acts 1:5; 1 Corinthians 12:13). The gospel of salvation was preached to the Jew first (Romans 1:16), until the larger part of that nation rejected the message. Then it was sent to the Gentiles (all who are not Jews), and God began to *visit the Gentiles, to take out of them a people for his name* (Acts 15:14).

Since the day of Pentecost, this has been God's program. He is saving *whosoever will* from every kindred, tribe, and nation and making them members of His Church by the working of His blessed Holy Spirit who places each of them into the Body of Christ.

Now it is important to notice that the Dispensation of Grace began before the Church Age (the Cross was fifty days prior to Pentecost) and lasts after the Church Age (which ends at the Rapture). While the Church Age ends at the Rapture, the Dispensation of Grace does not end until Christ returns to earth to set up His glorious Kingdom.

It is also of utmost importance to keep clearly before us that Israel was not the Church. Neither is the Church an outgrowth of, or a sect of Israel. It is a wholly new thing, hidden in ages past but now revealed, first by Christ Himself and then by His New Testament apostles and prophets (Ephesians 3:1-10).

The implications of this distinction are multitude and Dr. Renald Showers addresses them with his typical care and clarity when he writes, "It should be noted that the Covenant Theology view of the nature of the Church (i.e., that the Church is an extension of Israel [my note]), leads logically to several false conclusions. Israel and the Church are the same; there are no distinctive groups of saints throughout history; all saints of all periods of history are members of the Church; since saints will be on earth during the Tribulation period, the Church will be on earth during the Tribulation, and there will be one general resurrection of dead saints at one time, not more than one resurrection of saints at different times." [1]

As can be clearly seen, understanding the distinction between the Church and Israel is no small matter. It will determine much of your understanding concerning what the Church is and what it should do, and it will certainly determine your understanding of events in the future. As Dr. John MacArthur has so well put it, "Dispensationalism is the distinction between Israel and the Church." [2]

Looking again at the chart, the Church Age is indicated by the seven lamps on the steps. These represent the seven churches addressed in Revelation chapter two and three, but also they represent the seven stages of development during the Church Age and I will examine them more fully later on.

The Rapture is indicated by the two arrows, one ascending and one descending, which point to the cloud which is labeled "1 Thessalonians 4:17." The word Rapture (from the Latin Rapto), means "to be caught up." It is translated from the Greek *harpadzo* (to seize - catch away, up, pluck, take by force), and that is exactly what happens to the Church when it is completed.

According to 1 Thessalonians 4:13-18 and 1 Corinthians 15:51-57, Christ will come **in the air** (not to the earth at this time) and resurrect the sleeping saints, and catch them up to meet Him in the air. Those who are saved and still living here on earth will be miraculously changed and caught up with the others, *and so shall we ever be with the Lord.*

After this event, which ends the Church Age, you will see from the chart that the Dispensation of Grace continues for seven more years, which is noted on the chart by the word "WRATH." This covers the seven-year period that follows the Rapture of the Church and the end of the Church Age. So, you see that while the Church Age takes place within the Dispensation of Grace, the two are not identical.

Now I would like to do a brief overview of this entire dispensation, referring again to the chart. Beginning immediately after the Cross, we come to the ascension of Christ from the Mount of Olives, noted by the arrow and the verse, Acts 1:9.

Then the Church Age begins on the day of Pentecost, noted by the descending arrow labeled "Acts 1:4, 5, and 1 Corinthians 12:13." This indicates the descent of the Holy Spirit as promised by Jesus in John 14:16-18, 26; 15:26, 27; 16:7-15, and the reference to 1 Corinthians 12:13, indicates the coming of that Baptism which forms the Church, the Body of Christ.

In the center of the Church Age, under the word "GRACE" on the chart, you will see the word "MYSTERY." This word appears frequently in the New Testament, and it is important that we know what it means. I defer to the definition given by Dr. C. I. Scofield:

> "A mystery in Scripture is a previously hidden truth, now divinely revealed, but in which a supernatural element still remains despite the revelation" [3]

Now under the word MYSTERY, there are three references given; the first is "Matthew 16:18," which is Jesus' declaration *I will build my Church.* The second is "1 Corinthians 12:13," which defines how the Church came into existence, and "Ephesians 3:1 - 10," affirming that the Church was a Mystery in ages past. Concerning this Dr. Scofield writes:

> That Gentiles were to be saved was no mystery (Rom.9:24-33; 10:19-21). The mystery "hidden in God" was the divine purpose to make of Jew and Gentile a wholly new thing—"the Church, which is his

[Christ's] body," formed by the baptism with the Holy Spirit (1 Cor. ' 12:12-13) and in which the earthly distinction of Jew and Gentile disappears (Eph.2:14-15; Col. 3:10-11). The revelation of this "mystery" of the Church was foretold but not explained by Christ (Mt416:18). The details concerning the doctrine, position, walk, and destiny of the Church were committed to Paul and his fellow "apostles and prophets by the Spirit" (Eph.3:5). 4

Turning now to Christ's "Second Coming," Dispensationalists have taken a lot of criticism for teaching what has been called a 2-stage second coming, that is, Christ coming first in the air to receive the Church to Himself, and seven years later coming to the earth with the Church to set up His Kingdom. Some have supposed that Dispensationalists are teaching two second comings, or a second and third coming. A closer look will show that we are not.

At the Rapture, you will see by comparing the Scriptures regarding each event that Christ does not come to the earth but in the air, and we are caught up to meet Him, whereas at the Revelation we come with Him, and He does come to the earth. At the Rapture He comes as a Bridegroom to claim His Bride (the Church), at His Revelation (*apokalupsis*: 2 Thessalonians 1:7), He comes *in flaming fire taking vengeance on those who know not God.* That is not the way a Bridegroom comes for a Bride. There are many other contrasts to these two events.

Finally, please notice the period labeled "WRATH." A reading of the verses will make you familiar with this section. Actually the whole book of Revelation, from chapter 4:1 to chapter 19:21, deals with this period. It should be noted that the word "Church" does not appear anywhere in these chapters and I believe that is simply because the Church is no longer on earth during that period, but in heaven.

The reference to "the saints" in the Tribulation should not confuse us. There have been "saints" in every age. The "saints" of the Tribulation period are those who are saved after the Rapture of the Church (Revelation 7:4 – 14).

As we review this dispensation, you will notice again the often-repeated pattern. The dispensation begins by a gracious act of God, followed by failure on the part of man, and ending in judgment.

The cross opened the way for grace. In the last chapter we looked at the verse on the left side of the cross, Galatians 3:13, *Christ hath redeemed us from the curse of the law, being made a curse for us.* We saw how Christ answered every claim for judgment which the law made against us.

In Colossians 2:14, Paul says that *the handwriting of ordinances* (the law) was *against us.* It was *against us* because the essential nature of the law and the nature of men are at opposite poles. The law is holy and just and good. Man is sinful and defiled and evil. Because man is what he is by nature, he cannot keep God's holy law even when he wants to (Romans 7:14-24 and 8:7, 8). Because the law demands obedience, which man cannot produce, and curses the disobedience which man does produce, the law is against us.

Now notice what Christ did with *the handwriting of ordinances that was against us, and which was contrary to us.* Colossians 2:14 says He *Blotted out... and took it out of the way, nailing it to His cross.* What a picture! Christ, as God saw him, had over his head, not the accusation of Pilate, *This is Jesus of Nazareth, the King of the Jews,* but the accusation of a broken Law.

All that the Law condemned and cursed, against all of the sin of all of the world, was hung over the head of Christ along with the verdict, *The wages of sin is death,* and Jesus paid in full! So the Cross makes it possible for God to deal with the whole human race in grace because it answered every charge a holy God, or a just law could make against us.

I believe it may be important here to think about how grace operates. Grace is the unmerited favor of God bestowed upon an undeserving sinner. It is God giving us what we do not deserve. Now what is it that God gives? *The gift of God is eternal life, through Jesus Christ our Lord* (Romans 6:23). God gives us salvation when we deserve condemnation - that is grace.

However, since grace is undeserved and unmerited, it is obvious that we cannot earn it. If we could, it would become our due and cease at once to be grace (Romans 4:4). How then can we receive it? Listen to what God says, *But to him that worketh not, but believeth on him that justifieth the ungodly, his faith is counted* (put to his account as) *for righteousness* (Romans 4:5). So when we acknowledge our lost condition and look to God in faith to forgive and save us without a single work or act on our part, we are saved forever and given eternal life (Romans 5:1; 10:13; Ephesians 2:8, 9; 2 Timothy 1:9; 1 John 5:11, 13).

I remember well the first time I purchased a small offset printing press. I had never used that kind of press before and after purchasing it, I asked the dealer what I needed to know in order to operate it. I will never forget his answer. He said simply, "Oil doesn't mix with water." While that answer was woefully short of telling me what I needed to know to operate the press, he had placed his finger on the very thing that makes offset printing possible. Oil and water do not mix.

It is just so with Law and Grace or works and grace. In Romans chapter eleven Paul gives us the same answer regarding works and grace: *And if by grace, then is it no more of works: otherwise grace is no more grace. But if it be of works, then is it no more grace: otherwise work is no more work* (Romans 11:6).

Grace is a gift. As soon as we do one thing to earn it, it ceases to be a gift and therefore is no longer grace (Romans 11:6). A gift must be received, not earned. Since salvation is something that is spiritual and invisible, something you can neither see nor touch, you must receive it by believing that it is yours. You believe that Christ died for your sins personally, died in your place as your substitute, and you believe that you are thereby freed from guilt and forgiven; your debt is paid and God is satisfied; and you rest and rejoice in that assurance - you are saved.

What did you do? Nothing! You only believed that Christ really did what God says He did and that you are forgiven because He did. Read slowly: John 1:12, 29; 3:14, 18, 36; 5:24; 6:28, 29, 35; 14:1; 20:30, 31.

But grace cannot operate apart from faith. Paul says, *Therefore it is of faith, that it might be by grace* (Romans 4:16). Faith means putting our whole confidence in Christ and Christ alone for our salvation. And just as grace and works cannot be mixed, neither can grace and the law. Thus the contrasts between the essential nature of the Dispensation of Law and the Dispensation of Grace are ubiquitous. I close this chapter with an excerpt from C. I. Scofield's little booklet, Rightly Dividing the Word of Truth:

> "It is...of the most vital moment to observe that Scripture never, in any dispensation, mingles these two principles (of law and grace).... Law is God prohibiting and requiring. Grace is God beseeching and bestowing. Law is a ministry of condemnation; grace, of forgiveness. Law curses, grace redeems from that curse. Law kills; grace makes alive. Law shuts every mouth before God; grace opens every mouth to praise Him. Law puts a great and guilty distance between man and God. Grace makes guilty man nigh to God. Law says, 'Do and live.' Grace says, 'Believe and live.' The mingling of them (these two principles) in much of the current teaching of the day spoils both; for law is robbed of its terror, and grace of its freeness" 5

CHAPTER TWELVE:
THE DISPENSATION OF GRACE
– *The Dispensation Analyzed*

In this chapter we will again analyze the dispensation using the key words that should be familiar to you by now. Because this is the dispensation in which we are living, we will look at it more in depth and our analysis will carry over into chapter thirteen as well.

RESPONSIBILITY
It is because God offers to all men everywhere forgiveness and salvation on the basis of Christ's death in their place on the cross that we call this period, the Dispensation of Grace. Two observations are very important:

First, God's free forgiveness to believing sinners is perfectly just (Romans 3:25, 26). If Christ died for me, and I by faith accept His death as mine (Galatians 2:20), then the law of double jeopardy insures me against having to face judgment against my sins at a future time. Since Christ died in my place, God reckons it as my death and:

> *Payment He will not twice demand,*
> *First at my bleeding Surety's hand,*
> *And then again at mine.* [1]

He that heareth my words, and believeth on him that sent me, HATH everlasting life, and <u>shall not come into condemnation, but is passed from death unto life</u> (John 5:24).

Secondly, since salvation is now offered to all men on the basis of faith, it now becomes the responsibility of all men to accept God's gracious offer and believe. The sin question was settled at Calvary. It is now the Son question - What will you do with Jesus? Those who believe are *not condemned,* but by the fact of the responsibility man now has to believe, those who believe not are *condemned already because he hath not believed in the name of the only begotten Son of God* (John 3:18).

The work of the Holy Spirit during this age is not primarily to convict the world of sins (the law does that), but to convict the world of the one sin of unbelief (John 16:9). The *sin which doth so easily beset us,* spoken of by the writer of Hebrews (Hebrews 12:1), is none other than the sin of unbelief. (See also Hebrews 2:1-3; 3:12, 18, 19; 4:2, 11; 10:26.)

This is the age of sowing and reaping. The Word of God is sown in the hearts of men, and as they respond, so they are judged (Matthew 13:1-23). The responsibility of the Christian is to get the message out to a lost world. The responsibility of all who hear is to believe.

The payment for sin which Christ made at Calvary satisfied God's justice, and since God is satisfied it is of no importance whatever that moralists or unbelievers or sacramentalists of all sorts are not satisfied. The question to ask is, "Am I satisfied with the death Christ died on the cross in my place, and am I resting all my hopes of heaven on Him?"

RESTRICTION
All things are lawful for me (1 Corinthians 10:23). Now that is a very striking statement, and one that many find difficult to believe; nevertheless it is God's Word. The rest of the verse goes on to explain that *all things are not expedient* (profitable, helpful). This

leads us to one of the greatest debates of the Dispensation of Grace – how is the redeemed believer sanctified? Or, to ask it another way, what is the controlling principle of life in this dispensation?

To answer that question we need to carefully examine what Paul tells us in Romans 7:1-6. Paul uses the analogy here of marriage. A woman who is married is bound by the marriage covenant to her husband for as long as he lives. His readers would understand that and immediately agree. As long as she was bound by the covenant, the only way she could be free to lawfully marry another would be if her husband died.

Now Paul begins to draw the application. We were "married" (i.e., in covenant relationship), to the law. When Paul uses that term, he is referring to the entire Mosaic Law, the Law made with Israel at Mount Sinai. But when we trusted Christ, God reckons us to have died with Christ. Hence, death has occurred – we are dead and our former covenant relationship to the law is now broken.

Furthermore, Christ not only died – He rose again. We are risen with Him and therefore free to enter into a new relationship – we may now be legally "married" to Christ. We have therefore, no further obligation to our former husband, for we are dead to that relationship forever.

Paul strongly intimates that the purpose of the marriage union is to *"bring forth fruit"* (Romans 6:21; 7:5). But that could not happen in union with our former husband "the Law." The fault, of course, was not in the Law but in us; *the motions of sins, which were by the law, did work in our members to bring forth fruit unto death.* The picture is not a pretty one. Because of the disease of sin that was in us, and was only aggravated by the Law, our union with the Law always resulted in a still-born child (*fruit unto death*).

But now we are in union with Christ, our new husband. So what brings forth the fruit of children in a marriage? The love-life of the husband and wife! What brings forth the living fruit of righteousness in the life of the believer? His love-life with Christ!

The more the believer abides in Christ and seeks union with Him, the more fruit is produced through that union.

Finally, notice how this teaching further implies that just as our former union to the Law could only be broken by death, so our union with Christ can only be broken by death. But since, *Christ being raised from the dead dieth no more; death hath no more dominion over him.* (Romans 6:9) In short, the implication is that our union with Christ is eternal and can never be broken, and that of course, is the teaching of Scripture – we are indeed eternally secure.

So when we were saved, we not only died to the Law and its jurisdiction over us, but we were made alive to Christ (Romans 6:8-11). We became united to Him forever, and it is then wrong to ever return to our old husband – the law. Thus, Paul argues that we as believers are *not under the law* (Romans 6:14). This brings us to the verse on the chart under Restriction.

The objection might be raised, and often is, "Isn't that teaching "lawlessness? If you can be saved simply by faith / believing and never lost again, you could do anything that you pleased. You could live like the devil and still go to heaven." Such a statement demonstrates a total blindness to a true work of grace, but in order to discover the truth, we will examine it in the light of the Word of God.

God declares that we are saved by grace (Ephesians 2:8, 9; Romans 4:5, 16). We have seen that the Law has nothing to do with our salvation and that after we are saved we are actually dead to the Law. Is the Christian then free to just "do as he pleases"? In a sense, yes - *All things are lawful for me.*

But there is one vital factor in this discussion which has been omitted and which changes the whole equation. That is the truth that, *If any man be in Christ, he is a new creature; old things are passed away; behold, all things are become new* (II Corinthians 5:17).

The Christian can do as he pleases because as long as he walks in communion with Christ, he pleases to do what pleases God. *God hath sent forth the Spirit of His Son into your hearts* (Galatians 4:6). The Spirit of God's Son is the Spirit which can say, *I do always those things that please the Father* (John 8:29). It can say, *My meat is to do the will of Him that sent me and to finish His work* (John 4:34). It is the Spirit which is "well pleasing" to God.

Whenever someone says, "If you could be saved and eternally safe by grace alone you would live like the devil," he is only revealing that he knows nothing of the changed heart which grace produces. He would live like the devil because he loves the things which the devil loves, and he only does good because he is afraid of the consequences of sin. Such is not the case with the true Child of God.

Grace makes us see our own worthlessness and conquers the heart, the seat of the affection and will. It transforms us from God-hating rebels to God-loving saints. It creates in us a new heart so that we *do the will of God from the heart* (Ephesians 6:6; Jeremiah 24:7; Ezekiel 36:26, 27; 2 Corinthians 3:3; Galatians 4:6).

The whole attitude of the believer toward the law may be seen by a simple comparison. Civil law may forbid me to commit adultery under penalty of fine and imprisonment. But I have no need for such a law. My love for my wife teaches me the same thing far more effectively. The law may leave me with the desire and strong temptation to evil, but love makes me dead to its appeal.

Now the believer lives for Christ out of love for Him. Read carefully Galatians 5:22, 23. The Spirit of God's Son produces only those things which no law of man or of God would forbid. The whole usefulness of the Law is thus done away with - we are not under the Law.

Furthermore, God has provided for us the indwelling Spirit of God. The Spirit produces love (Galatians 5:22), guides love

(Galalatians 5:16), and empowers love (Romans 8:3, 4). Love is the fulfilling of the law (Romans 13:10). Love is described in 1 Corinthians 13 and is exemplified in Romans 5:6-8.

Love is the **royal law** and **the law of Christ** and is the believer's rule of life. Therefore, while all things are lawful for the believer, since he is not under the Law, yet all things are not expedient, since he is under love, and he is therefore not lawless, rather he is "in-lawed (made one of the family) to Christ".

In this Dispensation of Grace, true love, produced, guided and empowered by the Holy Spirit who lives in the heart of every believer is the Christian's "rule of life". All that the law demanded, *the love of God shed abroad in our hearts by the Holy Ghost* (Romans 5:5) produces.

Love will do only that which is helpful and profitable; that which is *expedient* and so, while under no restriction as such, the believer is governed by the life within which has made him a new creature... *And as many as walk according to this rule, peace be on them...* (Galatians 6:16).

RELATIONSHIP
As we begin to examine the believer's relationship to God in this dispensation, it would be helpful to recall something of the relationship of believers during the past dispensations. Only in the first did man enjoy direct fellowship with God. In the second he approached God though sacrifice, acting as his own priest. The practice during the third was for the king or ruler to act as mediator and priest on behalf of his subjects. In the Dispensation of Promise, we find that responsibility being borne by the family patriarch. Under Law, it was through the Aaronic Priesthood.

The purpose of Christ's sacrifice on the cross was to bring man, who by nature was at enmity with God, from enmity to amity. The word translated enmity in the New Testament means "to hate someone, or to be the enemy of someone." This was precisely our attitude toward God until we were saved, as Romans 8:7, 8 clearly states: *Because the carnal mind is enmity against God: for it is not subject to the law of God, neither indeed can be. So then they that are in the flesh cannot please God* (See also Romans 3:9-18).

Paul's description of his ministry found in 2 Corinthians 5:18-20, implies man's former enmity toward God.

> *And all things are of God, who hath reconciled us to himself by Jesus Christ, and hath given to us the ministry of reconciliation; To wit, that God was in Christ, reconciling the world unto himself, not imputing their trespasses unto them; and hath committed unto us the word of reconciliation. Now then we are ambassadors for Christ, as though God did beseech you by us: we pray you in Christ's stead, be ye reconciled to God.*

Reconciliation is accomplished when Christ, who has put away sin (the source of enmity), by the sacrifice of Himself, receives the believing sinner and presents him to the Father, forgiven and made new. It is Christ's taking the hand of the believing sinner and the hand of the Father and clasping the two hands together.

This is the first step of our new relationship under grace, according to Colossians 1:21, 22; *And you, that were sometime alienated and enemies in your mind by wicked works, yet now hath he reconciled in the body of his flesh through death, to present you holy and unblameable and unreproveable in his sight.*

Notice how different this is from the Law. Since the *law made nothing perfect* (Hebrews 7:19), its function was to put a great and guilty distance between man and God. But the sacrifice of Christ rent the veil and opened the new and living way (Hebrews 10:19-22) so that we are now nigh unto God, as one has put it:

> So dear, so very dear to God,
> More dear I cannot be;

> The love wherewith He loves His Son,
> Such is His love to me.
>
> So near, so very near to God,
> Nearer I could not be,
> For in the person of His Son,
> I am as near as He. 2

This then, brings us to the second phase of our new relationship; namely our perfect standing in Christ. Since the sacrifice of Calvary was a perfect sacrifice - that is, it perfectly and completely accomplished the purging of sins - those who come under the benefits of Christ's sacrifice, through faith, are perfectly cleansed, and endowed with the perfect righteousness of Christ, therefore perfect in their standing before God.

The believer may be saved for fifty years and live a conscientious and godly life, serving Christ with all his heart, but as far as his standing before God is concerned he was just as perfect the moment he was saved as he is today. The reason for this is that we cannot add anything to Christ's work. Christ made a perfect sacrifice, which perfectly takes away sin, and saved us perfectly, and we are, therefore, perfect in Him.

Since our position depends not on what we are or do, but on what He has done for us, it is eternal and changeless. Dr. C. I. Scofield's booklet, "Rightly Dividing the Word of Truth," has an excellent chapter on this subject entitled "The Believer's Standing and State," in which he says;

> "A prince, when still a little child, is as stubborn and self-willed as other little children. On one day he may be obedient and teachable and loving; he is then happy and receives approval. On the next, he may be rebellious, self-willed, and disobedient, and then he is unhappy and perhaps disciplined. But he is just as much a

prince on the second day as on the first. Hopefully, as time goes on, he will learn to behave as he should. He will then become more princely, but not more really a prince. He was born a prince." 3

Now I want to look at the verse we used on the chart opposite "Relationship," 1 Peter 2:9, which reads; *But ye are a chosen generation, a royal priesthood, an holy nation, a peculiar people; that ye should shew forth the praises of him who hath called you out of darkness into his marvellous light.*

What a difference that is from a very similar passage found in Exodus 19:5, 6 where we read; *Now therefore, if ye will obey my voice indeed, and keep my covenant, then ye shall be a peculiar treasure unto me above all people: for all the earth is mine: And ye shall be unto me a kingdom of priests, and an holy nation.*

Now please notice the difference in these two passages. The passage in Exodus begins, *if ye will . . . then ye shall be.* In other words the proffered position was conditional and depended upon obedience. This, by the way, is the reason Israel never attained it.

However, in contrast to that, Peter writes, *But ye are.* No conditions to that. What the law offered conditionally, grace imparted freely. So the believer's position in this dispensation is a gift by grace.

Having given us such a high and holy position, we are exhorted to walk in the light of our exalted standing, and so the verse continues, *. . .that ye should show forth the praises of him who hath called you out of darkness into his marvelous light.* But notice again there is no "if" that is, the promise is not conditional. We attain our new relationship by grace through faith alone.

Looking at the verse we now see what our standing or position in Christ includes."'

- *A Chosen Generation* - that is, we possess a new life (compare John 1:12, 13; 2 Corinthians 5:17; 1 John 5:11, 12).

- *A Royal Priesthood* - that is, we possess a new service (compare Romans 12:1, 2; Hebrews 13:15, 16).

- *A Holy Nation* - that is, we have a new citizenship (compare John 17:14-16; James 4:4; 1 John 2:15-17).

- *A Peculiar People* - that is, we have a new identity. The word "peculiar" literally means, *a people for his own possession.* We belong to Him! [4]

Thus we see something of the believer's relationship with God in this dispensation. It is an exalted position and because it is, let us *walk worthy of the Lord* (Colossians 1:10).

In the next chapter we will complete our analysis of the Dispensation of Grace by looking at man's Ruination, God's Reckoning and God's gracious and glorious Remedy.

CHAPTER THIRTEEN:
THE DISPENSATION OF GRACE
-The Failure – Apostasy

- "Of course I do not believe in the virgin birth, or in that old-fashioned substitutionary doctrine of the atonement; and I do not know any intelligent Christian minister who does" [1]

- "Jesus must have been the child of a German soldier" [2]

- "The Virgin Birth is a Myth which churchmen should be free to accept or reject" [3]

- *Now the birth of Jesus Christ was on this wise: When as his mother Mary was espoused to Joseph, before they came together, she was found with child of the Holy Ghost* (Matthew 1:18).

The preceding are four statements made by different men concerning the birth of Christ. The first three are statements by recent clergymen - each of them prominent men by earth's standards. The last is the inspired writing of the Apostle Matthew. As you can see, the first three are completely contradictory to the last.

The first three suggest that Jesus Christ was an illegitimate – born of fornication. The last declares that He was the Son of God, born of a virgin mother through the working of the Holy Spirit of God (read Luke's account; Luke 1:26-35). The first three represent that "spirit of apostasy" which the Bible everywhere asserts will dominate the last days of the Church Age immediately before the Rapture.

The word "apostasy" is transliterated from the Greek word *apostasia* which means "a falling away." Used in its specific theological sense it means a deliberate departure from the truth as revealed in the Old and New Testaments.

Notice that the devilish statements which we quoted in the introduction to this chapter constitute just that. The record of Matthew and Luke concerning Christ's birth is clear. These present-day apostate teachers simply refuse to believe it and so substitute their own rational (and radical) theories which deny the true nature and character of Jesus Christ.

The denial of the deity of Christ, His virgin birth and substitutionary death are not all that apostate teachers deny by any means. They deny the inspiration of the Scriptures (2 Timothy 3:16).

> "I let go of the Bible as a divine product. I learned that it is a human culture product. . .I realized that whatever 'divine revelation' and 'inspiration of the Bible' meant (if they meant anything), they did not mean that the Bible was a divine product with divine authority." [4]

They deny the substitutionary death of Jesus Christ on the cross in our behalf (Romans 4:25; 2 Corinthians 5:21; 1 Peter 2:24).

> "A common belief in the atonement presents a God who is incapable of forgiving unless He kicks someone else." [5]

> "The Church's fixation on the death of Jesus as the universal saving act must end. Substitution was the name of this vile doctrine." [6]

> "The God who exacts the last drop of blood from His Son, so that His just anger, evoked by sin, may be appeased ... This God does not exist." [7]

They further deny the possibility of miracles (Acts 17:32); the bodily resurrection (1 Corinthians 15:12); the Second Coming (2 Peter 3:3, 4); and a host of other doctrines taught by Scripture.

Since belief, or faith, is the one responsibility of this dispensation, it is not surprising to see that this is the very place where Satan attacks and where man fails. Apostasy exchanges faith for unbelief!

We have noticed the same thing in each preceding dispensation. In the first, man was to obey a simple command; he failed through "disobedience." In the second, his conscience was to guide him, and *every imagination of the thoughts of his heart was only evil continually*. In the third, he was to form to a government that would rule for God, and he rebelled and deified himself.

And so goes the record through each of the following eras. Man always fails at the exact point at which he is being tested. This is a key concept and will help you greatly if you keep it in mind.

RUINATION

I charge thee therefore before God, and the Lord Jesus Christ, who shall judge the quick and the dead at his appearing and his kingdom; Preach the word; be instant in season, out of season; reprove, rebuke, exhort with all longsuffering and doctrine. For the time will come when they will not endure sound doctrine; but after their own lusts shall they heap to themselves teachers, having itching ears; And they shall turn away their ears from the truth, and shall be turned unto fables (2 Timothy 4:1-4).

Please note how clearly this verse shown on the chart indicates the condition of apostasy. This particular verse refers primarily to the temperament of the people and their demand for silken-tongued messengers of light (see also 2 Corinthians 11:13-15).

Tragically, this disposition to unbelief is nurtured by false teachers - in fact, it is instigated by them! (Acts 20:27-31; Galatians 1:6-9; 1 Timothy 4:1-3; 2 Timothy 3:1-5; 2 Peter 2:1-22; 1 John 4:1-6; 2 John 7-11; Jude 4).

Ironically, while these apostates depreciate and despise the inspired Word of God, they fulfill it by doing and teaching the exact things which the Word predicted they would. In a sense then, their actions validate the very Book they deny.

Now please refer again to the chart on page 81 at the beginning of this section. On the chart there are seven steps, and on each step there is a lamp. These lamps represent the seven churches of Revelation chapters 2 and 3.

Let me suggest that you read carefully the note on "the messages to the seven churches" found on page 1331 of the Scofield Reference Bible. It is included in the Appendix if you do not have an original Scofield Bible. (see Appendix pp. 205).

Notice that the steps go down during the age. This is, indeed, the general trend, although the churches of Sardis and especially of Philadelphia certainly present some improvement over the preceding ones.

In the message to the last church, Laodicea, we find Christ standing outside His Church, knocking on the door for admittance, and that is the condition of things as the Church Age ends. The invitation is an individual one (Revelation 3:20-22), signifying that the Church as a whole is apostate, but individuals within that group can *open the door* and have personal fellowship with Christ.

These churches thus form a chronological, prophetic picture of the course of the whole Church Age. Each of the names is significant, as are the key phrases in the message. These key phrases are noted on the chart under each church. The periods they represent are also noted.

Now a few words about Apostates – Apostates are those who have willfully rejected revealed truth. Jesus said that these false teachers would come unto you as *wolves in sheep's clothing* (Matthew 7:15).

A "sheep" in Scripture stands for a true believer (John 10), so these men will appear to be true believers, but will, in reality, be apostate "wolves." They will not come wearing signs that say, "I am an apostate." They will come, rather, claiming to be true servants of God. They will be "injured" at the suggestion that they are in reality servants of Satan.

With tongues that are smoother than oil and with profound reasonings they will deceive the unwary. They are full of duplicity. They use the language of the Bible, but they invest it with their own perverse meanings so that the unwary are caught in the trap of deception. In the end, those who follow them will be caught in the pathos of an empty profession and awaken too late to the fact that they are lost! (Matthew 7:21-23).

How can the church guard against Apostates? First, each believer must know the teachings of the Bible (Bible doctrine), and he must know why these teachings are important. Secondly, believers, both individually and corporately (as churches), must demand a clear-cut stand on the essentials of the faith by the men who stand before them as teachers of the Word.

Apostasy is a willful act of rebellion, and we can be sure that God will answer it with judgment. At the height of this apostasy, Christ will take His true Church out of the world in the rapture. Then will follow His awful reckoning with those who were false professors but who did not really believe.

With almost monotonous redundancy, the pendulum of time has swung from God's gracious intervention and blessing on man to

God's righteous indignation and wrath toward man and back again. Five times the pendulum has swung, and five times the hammer blow of wrath has fallen. Today, it is about to fall again. Each succeeding blow has become more severe; and so as the sixth comes, it is nearly all the old world can stand. When the seventh falls, the world will utterly disintegrate and a new heaven and new earth will emerge (2 Peter 3:12, 13).

One basic principle is evident - God's goodness rejected always brings judgment. Until now man had rejected the voice of inspired men - prophets, foretellers, men of God. But those who are unbelieving during this age will reject the God-man, Jesus Christ. As the privilege has been greater, and the responsibility heavier, so the judgment is more severe (see Luke 20:9-18; Hebrews 2:1-4).

RECKONING
Scripture everywhere testifies that there is to be a period of great judgment at the end of this age. Jesus called it, *Great Tribulation, such as was not since the beginning of the world to this time, no, nor ever shall be* (Matthew 24:21). Jeremiah called it, *The time of Jacob's trouble* (Jeremiah 30:7; drawing attention to its importance to Israel). And John called it, *The hour of temptation, which shall come upon all the world, to try them that dwell upon the earth* (Revelation 3:10).

The following verses refer to this period and should be read carefully and thoughtfully: Isaiah 2:19; 24:1, 3, 6, 19-23; 26:20, 21; Jeremiah 30:1-7; Daniel 12:1; Joel 1:14-2:11; Amos 5:16-20; Zephaniah 1:14-18; Matthew 24:21, 22; Luke 21:25, 26; 1 Thessalonians 5:3; Revelation 6:15-17. It will be seen from these verses that the Great Tribulation is a fact and that it is characterized by great Wrath!

Not only is it a period of unprecedented human misery and satanic activity, but *God has a controversy with the nations*; God is angry, and it is the period of *The Wrath of the Lamb*. Notice that on the chart opposite "RECKONING," the reference includes from Revelation 4-20, indicating that this entire section of the book of Revelation describes this terrible period.

Reasons for The Tribulation

As we noted in our introduction to this chapter, every dispensation has resulted in man's failure and God's subsequent judgment of that failure. The Dispensation of Grace, therefore, is no exception. We have seen that this dispensation (and particularly the Church Age) will end in a time of unparalleled apostasy and willful rejection of the truth. The true Church will be raptured and the Church Age will end.

Left here on earth will be that great apostate system that claims to be God's church. This system, headed up by Antichrist, is referred to in Scripture as *MYSTERY, BABYLON THE GREAT, THE MOTHER OF HARLOTS AND ABOMINATIONS OF THE EARTH* (Revelation 17:5). She will be comprised of all kinds of false religious systems including an apostate Roman Catholicism, and apostate Protestantism, along with all of the false sects of Christendom and paganism united together.

No wonder her spiritual name is "Babylon" (i.e. Babel or confusion)! God will judge this great pretender as Revelation 17-19 reveals, and He will judge the nations that were cohorts with her.

Therefore, the first reason for the tribulation will be to *try them that dwell upon the earth* – those ungodly peoples who have rejected God and His Christ, and have accepted the rule of Antichrist and the apostate Babylonian Harlot instead (Revelation 8:13; 14:8-11; 16:2, 10, 19-21).

However, there is another reason for the Tribulation, and that reason has to do with God's program for Israel. As the former dispensation ended, the Jewish people rejected Jesus as their promised Messiah. The official answer of the nation regarding Him is found in John 19:15, *But they cried out, Away with him, away with him, crucify him. Pilate saith unto them, Shall I crucify your King? The chief priests answered, We have no king but Caesar.* And all through this Church Age, they have been enemies of the gospel. But a new day is about to dawn for Israel.

First, Israel is a nation again after an exile which lasted over 2,000 years. This is according to God's promises (Jeremiah 32:37-41). Although she is still dwelling in unbelief, Paul reveals to us in Romans chapters 9-11, God's intention for Israel.

Briefly he teaches us that: (1) God chose Israel by an act of sovereign grace, (2) He tried them under the Law and they failed, and (3) Because of their fall, salvation is now offered to the Gentiles. But (4) the Gentiles will also fall through unbelief, and (5) Israel will come to faith and salvation at last (see especially Romans 9:11, 31-33; 10:1-4; 11:1, 2, 13-32).

The primary part of this program - that is, Israel's return to faith and acceptance of Jesus as their individual Savior and their national Messiah - will come about during the tribulation period. Dr. J. Dwight Pentecost says, "God's purpose for Israel in the tribulation is to bring about the conversion of a multitude of Jews, who will enter into the blessings of the kingdom and experience the fulfillment of all Israel's covenants" (Deuteronomy 28:63-67; 30:1-6; Jeremiah 31:31-36; 33:24-26; Romans 11:26-29; Revelation 7:3-8). 8

It is not within the scope of our subject to develop how this will be accomplished. I deal with the question in depth in my book, ***The Prophetic Destiny of Israel & the Islamic Nations***. For now it is enough to see that God is going to bring the Jewish nation back to Himself and redeem them.

Not only will a vast number from Israel be saved, but *a great multitude, which no man could number, of all nations, and kindreds, and people, and tongues, stood before the throne, and before the Lamb, clothed with white robes, and palms in their hands* (Revelation 7:9). The tribulation will not only be a time of great suffering, but one of great salvation for unnumbered multitudes.

This does not lessen the terror of that awful period of wrath, but it should make us rejoice that our great God can accomplish such a glorious thing through such an awful time of trouble. The nature of this period is indescribably horrible, but it is the only alternative for a world that has rejected the Son of God.

REMEDY
For the Lord himself shall descend from heaven with a shout, with the voice of the archangel, and with the trump of God: and the dead in Christ shall rise first: Then we which are alive and remain shall be caught up together with them in the clouds, to meet the Lord in the air: and so shall we ever be with the Lord (1 Thessalonians 4:16, 17).

Gloriously, those who belong to Christ will not go through this period. God's remedy for us is the rapture (1 Corinthians 15:51-53; 1 Thessalonians 4:13-18).

There is no remedy for the Christ-rejecting world. The fact that we escape this period is indicated by the following verses:

> *Watch ye therefore, and pray always, that ye may be accounted worthy to escape all these things that shall come to pass, and to stand before the Son of man* (Luke 21:36)

> *For God hath not appointed us to wrath, but to obtain salvation by our Lord Jesus Christ* (1 Thessalonians 5:9).

> *Because thou hast kept the word of my patience, I also will keep thee from the hour of temptation, which shall come upon all the world, to try them that dwell upon the earth* (Revelation 3:10).

There are those who teach that the Church will go through this period of wrath, and others that it will go through part of it. Still others teach that some of the Church will go into the tribulation and others will not. Personally, I believe that there is abundant Scripture to indicate that the Church will be raptured before the tribulation.

Remember, the Church is a separate entity from Israel. God's program for the Church is different from His program with Israel. The Church began at Pentecost and it will end its program on earth at the Rapture. Then God will again begin that work which will ultimately bring Israel to faith in their Messiah, Jesus Christ, and allow Him to fulfill all of the Old Testament Covenant promises with that nation.

The tribulation which closes the Dispensation of Grace ends in the second coming of Christ to the earth to set up His Kingdom and reign. Revelation 19 deals with the events of this period. In our next chapter we will see how Christ's coming relates to the final dispensation: "The Dispensation of the Kingdom."

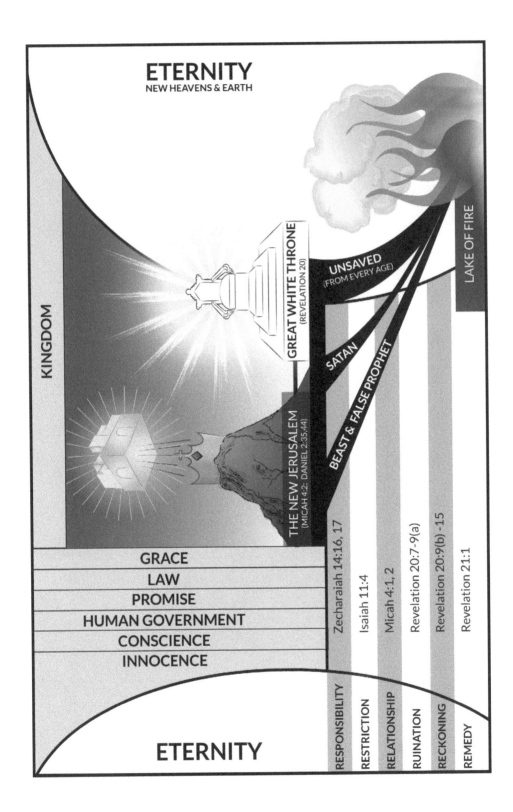

CHAPTER FOURTEEN:
THE DISPENSATION OF THE KINGDOM
– Reasons for the Kingdom

One of the questions frequently asked by non-dispensationalists is, "Why does there have to be a Millennium? What is the purpose of another thousand years?"

It is evident that from the writings preserved from the first and second centuries of the Christian era, the early Church Fathers were premillennial in their persuasion and believed and taught a literal earthly millennial Kingdom of Christ. But after the third century that persuasion began to change.

In St. Augustine's time, teaching concerning the Millennial Kingdom often focused entirely upon its earthly, material glory, and had become crass and power driven. The Church did what Israel had done – saw the Kingdom predictions wholly in the light of political aspirations, and that false concept repulsed the more spiritually minded. But that was not the whole story.

Augustine suffered from elements of Greek philosophic dualism that taught that anything of the material world was evil – only the spiritual could be pure. These factors, along with Augustine's own experiences of fleshly excess, (from which he was delivered by Divine grace), caused him to reject the entire idea of a literal earthly Kingdom. But to do that, he had to reinterpret vast amounts of prophetic Scripture to allow for this "adjustment."

Augustine, like Origen before him, began reinterpreting the meaning of key words. "Zion" would no longer refer to the literal city of David or be used as a synonym for the earthly city of Jerusalem. Zion would now refer to heaven, the eternal home of Christians, hence the hymn writer would write, "We're marching to Zion, the beautiful city of God." In like manner, any reference to Jerusalem which looked into the future was to be taken not as a reference to the literal earthly Jerusalem, but rather, to "Jerusalem above," the heavenly city.

Jesus sitting on David's throne was reinterpreted to mean the throne in heaven where He now sits with His Father (never mind the fact that it is always referred to in Scripture as, "the Father's Throne"). The argument was, "what need is there that He sit on the literal Throne of David and rule on earth, since He is already fulfilling the prophecy by ruling from heaven?" And thus the process of "spiritualizing" as it was called, (and is still called), took place. But "spiritualizing" was nothing more than redefining words and the result was predictable.

There is an undeniable fact, that he who defines the terms controls the debate. The easiest way to get people to accept a new way of thinking is to reinterpret the words that defined the argument. Once they have accepted the new meanings, the rest is easy. Hence, the Biblical teaching of the earthly Millennial Reign of Christ became obscured by the very words meant to affirm it.

I have already addressed the dispensationalist's passion for literal-historic-grammatical interpretation. If such were insisted upon, no further explanation would be necessary, for there is abundant Scriptural evidence for an earthly kingdom over which Christ Himself will reign. But because of the present confusion, I think it might be helpful to answer the basic question asked before, "Why is an earthly Millennial Kingdom a necessity?" I would urge at least the following reasons:

Because God has Decreed that Man shall have Dominion over the Earth.

When God created man in His own image, He decreed that man should have dominion over all of creation. (Genesis 1:26, 28). The Dominion decree of God is clearly repeated in Psalm 8 where David says,

> *When I consider thy heavens, the work of thy fingers, the moon and the stars, which thou hast ordained; What is man, that thou art mindful of him? and the son of man, that thou visitest him? For thou hast made him a little lower than the angels, and hast crowned him with glory and honour. Thou madest him to have dominion over the works of thy hands; thou hast put all things under his feet: All sheep and oxen, yea, and the beasts of the field; The fowl of the air, and the fish of the sea, and whatsoever passeth through the paths of the seas. O LORD our Lord, how excellent is thy name in all the earth* (Psalm 8:3 – 9).

This affirmation of God's purpose for man's dominion is referenced again in the New Testament book of Hebrews. Here the writer gives us a little further perspective:

> *For unto the angels hath he not put in subjection the world to come, whereof we speak. But one in a certain place testified, saying, What is man, that thou art mindful of him? or the son of man, that thou visitest him? Thou madest him a little lower than the angels; thou crownedst him with glory and honour, and didst set him over the works of thy hands: Thou hast put all things in subjection under his feet. For in that he put all in subjection under him, he left nothing that is not put under him. But now we see not yet all things put under him. But we see Jesus, who was made a little lower than the*

> *angels for the suffering of death, crowned with glory and honour* Hebrews 2:5 – 9)

In this passage the writer laments that man has not exercised the dominion over the earth that God intended, but expresses the confidence that he will do so, in the coming age, in the dominion of the Divine Man, Christ Jesus.

The phrase, *the world to come,* is defined by the writer's previous words in the concluding verses of chapter one, *Sit thou on my right hand until I make thine enemies thy footstool* (Hebrews 1:13). This phrase, taken from Psalm 2, speaks clearly of that time when the Father will give Christ the dominion over the entire earth including those who are His enemies. There is no way the verses of Psalm 110 can be construed to be referring to heaven, since Christ is said to be reigning in the midst of His enemies (Psalm 110:2). That is not a description of heaven where His enemies are all shut out.

So the first reason there must be a Millennium is to fulfill the Divine decree that man shall have dominion over the earth which finally occurs when Christ, the God-man reigns for a thousand years.

The Necessity to actuate what Peter called, "The Restoration of all things which God hath spoken by the mouth of His holy prophets."

> *Repent ye therefore, and be converted, that your sins may be blotted out, when the times of refreshing shall come from the presence of the Lord; And he shall send Jesus Christ, which before was preached unto you: Whom the heaven must receive until the times of restitution of all things, which God hath spoken by the mouth of all his holy prophets since the world began* (Acts 3:19 – 21).

Please note that the scope of this promise is limited by the phrase, *which God hath spoken by the mouth of His holy prophets;* thus it is not a promise that everyone will eventually be restored or saved as the Universalist would claim. What then is it that will be restored?

We can get a glimpse of what is in store by looking at just one chapter – the eleventh chapter of Isaiah (though the restoration is referenced in many places). In it we can discover at least five things which the prophets declared will be restored.

First, righteous judgment will be restored. The human heart longs for righteous judgment, but there is little to be had. Imagine, a justice system that will punish the guilty and acquit the righteous – how novel would that be? A judicial system that will know all the facts in every case, and will judge righteously with perfect judgment. In a world where few have every seen justice done, what a restoration that will be!

> *And there shall come forth a rod out of the stem of Jesse, and a Branch shall grow out of his roots: And the spirit of the LORD shall rest upon him, the spirit of wisdom and understanding, the spirit of counsel and might, the spirit of knowledge and of the fear of the LORD; And shall make him of quick understanding in the fear of the LORD: and he shall not judge after the sight of his eyes, neither reprove after the hearing of his ears: But with righteousness shall he judge the poor, and reprove with equity for the meek of the earth: and he shall smite the earth with the rod of his mouth, and with the breath of his lips shall he slay the wicked. And righteousness shall be the girdle of his loins, and faithfulness the girdle of his reins (Isaiah 11:1 – 5).*

Secondly, all nature will be restored to complete harmony with itself. Furthermore, man and nature will at last be in harmony with each other in a perfect relationship like that which existed in the Garden of Eden before the Fall.

> *The wolf also shall dwell with the lamb, and the leopard shall lie down with the kid; and the calf and*

> *the young lion and the fatling together; and a little child shall lead them. And the cow and the bear shall feed; their young ones shall lie down together: and the lion shall eat straw like the ox. And the sucking child shall play on the hole of the asp, and the weaned child shall put his hand on the cockatrice' den. They shall not hurt nor destroy in all my holy mountain: for the earth shall be full of the knowledge of the LORD, as the waters cover the sea* (Isaiah 11:6 – 9).

Thirdly, Gentiles will seek the King of Israel and peace will be restored among the nations.

> *And in that day there shall be a root of Jesse, which shall stand for an ensign of the people; to it shall the Gentiles seek: and his rest shall be glorious* (Isaiah 11:10).

Fourthly, national Israel will be completely restored to their ancient Land and all twelve tribes will be united together.

> *And it shall come to pass in that day, that the Lord shall set his hand again the second time to recover the remnant of his people, which shall be left, from Assyria, and from Egypt, and from Pathros, and from Cush, and from Elam, and from Shinar, and from Hamath, and from the islands of the sea. And he shall set up an ensign for the nations, and shall assemble the outcasts of Israel, and gather together the dispersed of Judah from the four corners of the earth. The envy also of Ephraim shall depart, and the adversaries of Judah shall be cut off: Ephraim shall not envy Judah, and Judah shall not vex Ephraim* (Isaiah 11:11 – 13).

Finally, Israel will be restored to victorious dominance over the surrounding nations. She will be completely restored to her ancient Land, even removing all the obstacles to Israel's final regathering.

> *But they shall fly upon the shoulders of the Philistines toward the west; they shall spoil them of the east together: they shall lay their hand upon Edom and Moab; and the children of Ammon shall obey them. And the LORD shall utterly destroy the tongue of the Egyptian sea; and with his mighty wind shall he shake his hand over the river, and shall smite it in the seven streams, and make men go over dryshod. And there shall be an highway for the remnant of his people, which shall be left, from Assyria; like as it was to Israel in the day that he came up out of the land of Egypt* (Isaiah 11:14 – 16).

And that is only one chapter of the prophets – there are many more such passages. The Millennium is necessary so that the restoration of all things foretold by the prophets may occur.

The Necessity to Silence the Claim that Man's reason for sinning rests outside himself in the conditions and environment that surround him.

Each of us is guilty of developing what some have called a "victim mentality." It's always someone else's fault. When Adam had eaten of the forbidden tree and God questioned him about his disobedience, his famous and classic response was, *The woman whom thou gavest to be with me, she gave me of the tree, and I did eat* (Genesis 3:12).

Adam was not the guilty party – he was a victim of the predilection of his wife. She was the one who desired the fruit – It was her fault that he sinned. And not only that, but it was God who had given her to Adam; so, it was really God's fault. And that shifting of the blame has continued throughout time and is classically expressed in comedian Flip Wilson's famous response, "The Devil made me do it."

Man has always blamed factors outside of himself for his sin. When crime is committed in the inner city, it is never the fault of the perpetrator, but always of his environment, his lack of education, his poverty, or a hundred and one other things outside of himself. He is not guilty – he is a victim.

The Millennial Kingdom will demonstrate the lie behind that rationalization. It will provide a perfect government with perfect justice and an environment with no one deprived or in want of any good thing. Education will at last be based on empirical truth not tainted with the lies of false philosophical systems such as humanism, evolution, or psycho-babble. Satan and his minions will be chained in the bottomless pit awaiting a future day of judgment (Revelation 20:2). In short, there will be no external factors to use as an excuse for sinning.

Still at the close of the Millennial period, a released Satan will find the fertile ground of corrupt human hearts ready to rebel against the King and His rule. The Millennial Kingdom will demonstrate that man's problem with sin is not external but internal - *The heart is deceitful above all things, and desperately wicked* (Jeremiah 17:9).

The Necessity to fulfill all the unfulfilled promises to National Israel

This reason alone could easily fill several chapters. One need only begin with the unconditional covenants to Abraham, found in Genesis chapters 12, 13, 15, 17, and 22, to see that all that God promised in what He called, *an everlasting covenant*, has not been fulfilled.

Please further note, as I indicate in my previous book, ***The Prophetic Destiny of Israel and the Islamic Nations,*** that the original covenant, which we call the Abrahamic Covenant, was reaffirmed to Isaac (Genesis 17:19, 21; 26:3) and to Jacob (28:3, 4, 12 – 15; 35:11, 12) after him.

Furthermore, God referred back to that covenant every time He was about to deliver Israel, beginning with the deliverance from Egypt (Exodus 2:24; 6:8), to the frequent deliverances in the wilderness (Exodus 32:12, 13).

In Israel's darkest times, even when the judgment of God fell heavily upon her, God remembered the covenant (Isaiah 54:10; Micah 7:20). All future blessing of the nation was always based upon the covenant and not Israel's performance.

When we speak of the "unfulfilled promises to Israel," it might be helpful to consider a few.

- A time when both Israel (the northern kingdom) and Judah (the southern kingdom) will be reunited in the Land (Ezekiel 36:16 – 37:28).

- A time when all Israel shall be saved: *as it is written, There shall come out of Sion the Deliverer, and shall turn away ungodliness from Jacob: For this is my covenant unto them, when I shall take away their sins* (Romans 11:26, 27).

- A time when Israel shall say, *Blessed is He that cometh in the name of the Lord* (Matthew 23:39). This is Jesus' clear prediction that the time will come, when this nation (Israel) that has rejected Him, will embrace Him as Lord and King.

- A time when Israel will enjoy eternal peace and prosperity in the Land and the nations will come to Israel for blessing (Zechariah 14:16).

- A time when *out of Zion shall go forth the law, and the word of the LORD from Jerusalem* (Isaiah 2:3).

And many more promises – we have only touched the surface. When will these be actuated, when will they be fulfilled? The Millennial Kingdom is a time for the fulfillment of all the promises to Israel.

Simply because God has decreed that there shall be a Millennial Reign of His Son on earth.

> *And I saw thrones, and they sat upon them, and judgment was given unto them: and I saw the souls of them that were beheaded for the witness of Jesus, and for the word of God, and which had not worshipped the beast, neither his image, neither had received his mark upon their foreheads, or in their hands; and they lived and reigned with Christ a thousand years. But the rest of the dead lived not again until the thousand years were finished. This is the first resurrection. Blessed and holy is he that hath part in the first resurrection: on such the second death hath no power, but they shall be priests of God and of Christ, and shall reign with him a thousand years.* (Revelation 20:4, 6).

The Holy Spirit uses the phrase, *a thousand years*, six times in seven verses. Does it not seem that perhaps that is what He meant to convey when using such precise specificity? Did He not intend that phrase to be taken literally? I think the answer is obvious to the honest mind.

Furthermore, the Millennial Kingdom is an earthly Kingdom because in Daniel's interpretation of Nebuchadnezzar's vision of the great image, the Stone *cut out of the mountains without hands* smites the image (all previous Gentile kingdoms) *and became a great mountain, and filled the whole earth* (Daniel 2:35). A "mountain" in prophetic symbolism stands for a Kingdom. Hence, "The Stone," (Christ), will destroy all previous earthly kingdoms and His kingdom will be over all the earth – Yes, the earth.

Another reason we can be sure that the Millennial Kingdom happens on earth is because God tells us, that phase of the Kingdom will have an end. John says it quite clearly; *And when the thousand years are expired, Satan shall be loosed out of his prison...* (Revelation 20:7). There will be a time when the thousand year Kingdom of Christ will end in its Dispensational form.

Paul explains something of this in his great resurrection passage: *Then cometh the end, when he shall have delivered up the kingdom to God, even the Father; when he shall have put down all rule and all authority and power. For he must reign, till he hath put all enemies under his feet.* 1 Corinthians 15:24, 25).

After man's final rebellion and failure, and the Judgment of the Great White throne (Revelation 20:11-15), the final form of Christ's glorious Kingdom will take place in eternity upon a new heaven and a new earth. Although the earth phase ends with the destruction of the present earth (2 Peter 3:10 – 13), the Kingdom will not end in the sense that it now merges into eternity, even though the earthly period referred to so often in Scripture has, as all earthly things have, a termination.

With these five considerations, I believe we can see clearly the necessity of an earthly, Millennial reign of Messiah, Jesus Christ. We now want to examine the Government of the Kingdom.

> *And there were great voices in heaven, saying, The kingdoms of this world are become the kingdoms of our Lord, and of his Christ; and he shall reign for ever and ever* (Revelation 11:15).

In our study of the Dispensation of Human Government, we saw how God gave authority to man to rule for the glory of God. After man's failure, God dealt for a time with a single nation, Israel. Through this nation, He promised to rule the world in righteousness, but this promise was delayed through Israel's disobedience.

Then during the captivity in Babylon (see the chart), God revealed that He was going to place the authority for human rule in Gentile hands. In Daniel chapter 2, Daniel interprets a dream for Nebuchadnezzar in which God reveals that four great world empires will arise to rule the earth. The empires were symbolized by the vision of the great image. The Babylonian Empire was the head of gold, the shoulders and breast of silver suggested the Medo-Persian Empire. The belly and thighs represented Greece, and the legs represented the Eastern and Western divisions of the Roman Empire.

The Roman Empire has never really ended and now through the power of the Roman Church and such movements as the Common Market and the proposed "United States of Europe," the empire will once again live. When it comes, it will finally be controlled by the Antichrist himself.

Notice that the time period of these four great empires has extended from the captivity in Babylon until now and will last until the second coming of Christ. This period is denoted on the chart as *The times of the Gentiles* (Luke 21:24). Christ will end this period by His personal advent to this earth.

Daniel pictures this (Daniel 2:34, 35, 44, 45) as the Stone (Christ) cut out without hands which will smite the image (symbol of Gentile power) on its feet (final form of the fourth empire). Then this Stone will become a great mountain and fill the whole earth. This, of course, signifies that Christ's Kingdom will be absolute and universal.

The People of the Kingdom
Two kinds of people populate the Kingdom. There are, first of all, those resurrected and glorified saints of all ages who *reign with him a thousand years* (Revelation 20:6). Among this number will be the twelve apostles who *sit upon twelve thrones, judging the twelve tribes of Israel* (Matthew 19:28).

The second class of people will be those saints who entered the Kingdom from the tribulation period. These are, of course, in natural bodies, and unlike those glorified saints who reign with Christ, they will partake in the natural functions of life, including the begetting of children.

It is important to see that the final dispensation (the Dispensation of The Kingdom), Christ's personal presence and the presence of glorified saints, will nevertheless be an earthly dispensation. This Kingdom is on earth, and the normal functions of earth life will continue throughout the thousand years.

Israel and the Kingdom
The promises made by God that Israel would one day be the head of the nations and not the tail are irrevocable and will be fulfilled. At Christ's first coming, fulfillment was delayed when Christ was rejected; but this was foreseen by God, and it in no way frustrated the original intention. In fact, it implemented it by making Christ the atonement for the nation; thus setting God free to deal with them in grace and fulfill the promises made to the fathers, even though Israel did not in any way merit such grace.

According to Paul, *they* (Israel today) *are beloved for the fathers'* (Abraham, Isaac, Jacob) *sakes. For the gifts and calling of God are without repentance* (Romans 11:28, 29). When our Lord returns, He will rule and reign over all the earth from Jerusalem, and all worship will again be centered there (see Isaiah 2:1-4; 26:1, 2; Jeremiah 3:17; Joel 3:17-21; Zechariah 8:1-8). These verses indicate plainly the fulfillment of our Lord's prayer taught to His disciples so many years ago, *Thy kingdom come, Thy will be done on earth, as it is in heaven* (Matthew 6:10).

The Earth During the Millennium
The Bible reveals that the most wonderful change will take place as regards the earth during the Kingdom. The earth has for many thousands of years suffered under the curse of man's sin (Genesis 3:17-19). The ground has brought forth briers and weeds; animal life has been fierce and bloody – "red in tooth and claw."

Paul says that *the whole creation groaneth and travaileth in pain together until now* (Romans 8:22). Creation is groaning under the curse - a curse that has made her subject to change and decay. Not willingly has she suffered this indignity, *but by reason of him who hath subjected the same in hope.*

When Christ comes and our own redemption is complete (Romans 8:21, 23), then creation itself shall be set free. The following verses describe the result: Isaiah 11:1-9; 35:1-10; 40:4, 5; 65:25; Ezekiel 34:23-31; Romans 8:19-21.

Conclusion:
So we have seen the necessity of a Millennial Kingdom, the Government of the Kingdom, the people that will inhabit the Kingdom, Israel's role in the Kingdom, and the effects of the Kingdom upon the earth itself. In our next chapter, I want us to begin to analyze the Millennial Kingdom following the six analytical words we have used to analyze each of the former Dispensations.

CHAPTER FIFTEEN:
THE DISPENSATION OF THE KINGDOM
– *Analyzing the Final Dispensation*

Where is the center of the earth? If you were a draftsman, you might answer that it is the spot where all of the isometric lines converge across the diameter of the sphere. To a geographer the answer would be quite different. It would deal with land masses, population figures, and in general, the surface of the earth.

To us, however, the question concerns importance as to the purposes of God, and this makes it quite simple to answer. Israel is the center of the earth. It was near here that civilization first began. It is here that the whole world divides itself between East and West, North and South. It is here that the attention of the world is being focused in these last days. It is here that the battle of the ages will end the nearly 3,000 years of Gentile world dominion (*Times of the Gentiles*). It is here that Christ will reign, governing the nations of the world during the final 1,000 years of human history.

RESPONSIBILITY - (Please refer to the chart)
Zechariah 14:16, 17, tell us that during the Dispensation of the Kingdom, all nations will be required to keep the yearly Feast of Tabernacles at Jerusalem. Of course, complete obedience to the King is required and righteousness in all relationships and at every level.

Isaiah says of the King and His Kingdom:

> *But with righteousness shall he judge the poor, and reprove with equity for the meek of the earth: and he shall smite the earth with the rod of his mouth (for correction), and with the breath of his lips shall he slay the wicked. And righteousness shall be the girdle of his loins, and faithfulness the girdle of his reins* (Isaiah 11:4, 5).

Along with the general character of His Kingdom, which will be righteousness and peace, there is also this specific command that the nations observe the annual Feast of Tabernacles. The question of course is, Why this particular requirement?

The feast of Tabernacles is first introduced in Leviticus 23 along with six other annual feasts, each of which had both a commemorative and a prophetic significance. The Feast of Tabernacles was significant in that it was the last Feast on the Jewish calendar, and it is the last Feast to be fulfilled in its prophetic aspects.

Commemoratively it looks back to Israel's dwelling in tents and booths in the wilderness (Leviticus 23:43), but prophetically it looks forward to the time when God shall *tabernacle* among His people. It is fulfilled during the Millennium and will last on into eternity, as will be seen from Revelation 21:3.

When the feast was observed in Israel, every person dwelling in the land of Israel, whether Jew or stranger in the land, was required to, *keep the feast* (Deuteronomy 16:13-15). It was a symbol of subjection to Israel's king. How fitting then that this feast is the one chosen by God to be observed during the Millennium; first to commemorate God's dwelling among men, and secondly to recognize the sovereignty of Israel's King (Jesus Christ) as King of kings over all the earth.

Of course, since a variety of sacrifices where required during this Feast, this raises the question of animal sacrifices during the

Millennium in the new Millennial Temple. This has been a particularly controversial issue because a return to any kind of sacrificial system seems contrary to the letter and spirit of the Epistle to the Hebrews. Hebrews makes it plain that the old system of animal sacrifice is now done away by the once offered, never to be repeated blood sacrifice of Christ.

Dr. Scofield and many others have helpfully argued that the practice as restored in the Kingdom is commemorative, that is, it acts for the inhabitants of the Kingdom in much the same way as the Lord's Supper does today for the Church. As every Bible student knows, the Lord's Supper is not a re-offering of the body of Christ (as is taught by Rome), nor does it contribute to cleansing from sin, but is a "remembrance" of Jesus' *once offered* sacrifice until he comes.

Obviously it will be crucial during the Kingdom, as it is now, that no one ever forget the perfect sacrifice which Christ has made. These Millennial sacrifices then will once again speak of how His one offering made peace, took away sin, created fellowship, and was a sweet savor to God.

Not all Mosaic rituals are repeated in the Millennial Temple but some are, such as the Passover. Even our Lord said:

> *With desire I have desired to eat this passover with you before I suffer: For I say unto you, I will not any more eat thereof, until it be fulfilled in the kingdom of God* (Luke 22:15-16).

There is no High Priest in the prophesied Millennial Temple (since our Lord Jesus is the High Priest) but descendants of Zadok will minister before the Lord. While it is clear that *the blood of bulls and of goats cannot* (and did not) *take away sin* (Hebrews 10:4), they did, *sanctify to the purifying of the flesh* (Hebrews 9:13). In other words, they provided ceremonial purity for the worshippers. It seems clear that this function will be resumed in the Millennium. God is again dwelling among mortals and the issue of ceremonial purity is raised once again.

In his very insightful treatment of the subject, Dr. John C. Whitcomb points out that Egyptians and other foreigners will offer animal sacrifices during the Millennium (Isaiah 19:21, 56:6-7, 60:7, 66:21). Dr. Whitcomb observes, "These sacrifices in the Millennium represent no step backward nor a depreciation of the finished work of Christ on Calvary. Unregenerate hearts need the physical penalties and temporal judgment set forth by these sacrifices." 1

Concerning the worship in the Millennial Temple, Dr. David Larsen observes, "Christ's finished work is reflected in the absence of a veil, an approachable Holy of Holies, Christ as High Priest, no Feast of Weeks (or Pentecost) and in other departures and deviations from the Mosaic economy." 2

RESTRICTION
Isaiah 11:4 actually sets forth the King's method of ruling the earth. Dr. Pentecost says, "Any overt act against the authority of the King will be punished with physical death." 3

The King's power will be absolute and His knowledge complete and His judgment upon any outbreak of sin immediate. This will cause great rejoicing among the saints, but some who are born during this time and who will, as subsequent events will show, never really submit their hearts to King Jesus, will chafe under this restraint of their natural depraved desires. Remember that in any age, *the carnal mind is enmity against God, for it is not subject to the law of God, neither indeed can be* (Romans 8:7, 8; see also Psalm 2:8-12; Psalm 72; Jeremiah 31:29, 30).

RELATIONSHIP
The verse on the chart gives a beautiful picture of the relationship of the Millennial people to the King.

> *But in the last days it shall come to pass, that the mountain of the house of the LORD shall be established in the top of the mountains, and it shall be exalted above the hills; and people shall flow unto it. And many nations shall come, and say, Come, and let us go up to the mountain of the*

> *LORD, and to the house of the God of Jacob; and he will teach us of his ways, and we will walk in his paths: for the law shall go forth of Zion, and the word of the LORD from Jerusalem* (Micah 4:1, 2).

All Messiah wanted to be to Israel at His first advent He will be to the world during the golden Millennial Age. He will be *King, Counselor, Shepherd, Master, Sustainer, Lawgiver, Father, Prince of Peace, Wonderful.* In short, He will be to the world all that they need for life at its fullest, richest, and best (Isaiah 9:6, 7; Micah 4:1, 2).

The Millennium presented in Scripture is not a period of carnality as has been presented by some who have, because of this false concept rejected a literal Kingdom, but rather a time of great spiritual blessing as George Peters indicates in his three volume work, *The Theocratic Kingdom,* as cited by Pentecost. [4]

Peters, defending both a literal and a spiritual Kingdom writes, "This Kingdom, although visible with a world dominion, is also necessarily spiritual. This proposition is the more needed since we are charged with gross carnality, etc., because we insist on retaining the plain grammatical meaning assigned to the Kingdom in the Holy Scriptures. While a purely material, naturalistic Kingdom, without spirituality, is unscriptural, so likewise an entire spiritual Kingdom, without the sanctified union of the material or natural, is utterly opposed to the Word of God." [5]

RUINATION
The Scripture for this is seen on the chart as Revelation 20:7 – 9:

> *And when the thousand years are expired, Satan shall be loosed out of his prison, And shall go out to deceive the nations which are in the four quarters of the earth, Gog and Magog, to gather them together to battle: the number of whom is as the sand of the sea. And they went up on the breadth of the earth, and compassed the camp of the saints about, and the beloved city: and fire*

came down from God out of heaven, and devoured them.

In our study of the Restriction (absolute obedience to the King and no overt act of rebellion), we said that there will be some who will inwardly rebel even during this age of peace and plenty. When Jesus set forth the constitution for His Kingdom in the Sermon on the Mount (Matthew 5:1-7:12), He gave warnings to those who wanted to enter the Kingdom (Matthew 7:13-27).

The demanding standards of righteousness which Jesus insisted upon were galling to the religious leaders of His day who had become accustomed to slipping through the loopholes of the Law. At that time they were in power, so they crucified Jesus. During the Kingdom He will be in power, so those who would otherwise rebel will submit to avoid His wrath.

At the end of the 1,000 years, God will release Satan from his prison in the bottomless pit. Satan will go to the four corners of the earth and organize all those who, while giving outward obedience during the Millennium, have hated the King in their hearts.

Tragically, Scripture reveals that there will be a multitude of such, as numerous as the sands of the sea. Satan will deceive them with the hope of overthrowing the King and controlling the earth for their own selfish ends.

The question is sometimes raised as to who these people will be who rebel since only saved persons enter the Kingdom. The answer is simple; they are some who have been born during the thousand years, which points up this dramatic fact - godly parents and perfect environments do not make saved men. Only the new birth can make new men in any age!

The words *Gog and Magog,* are in this instance used figuratively since a number of considerations make it obvious that this is not the same event as that described in Ezekiel 38, 39. The words are used to indicate that the battle is motivated by the same sinful and rebellious plans and that just like the former event there will be great multitudes of people involved.

The rebellion will, of course, prove the ruination of man during this last period of testing. It will show that man is a rebel at heart and so wicked and implacable that not even the King in all His glory and greatness can soften him or make him submit to God. Man's heart is so hard that mercy cannot win him, and judgment cannot frighten him.

RECKONING

And they went up on the breadth of the earth, and compassed the camp of the saints about, and the beloved city: and fire came down from God out of heaven, and devoured them (Revelation 20:9).

These verses, shown on the chart, plainly set forth God's judgment on that great host of rebels who responded to Satan's deception and attacked the camp of the saints and the Holy City, *and fire came down from God out of heaven, and devoured them.*

This actually ends the Dispensation of the Kingdom and brings about the final judgment of all the lost of every age. Verse 11 indicates the destruction of the old heaven and earth (2 Peter 3:10-12) and the "setting" of the Great White Throne Judgment. There is no place to hide for, *the earth and the heaven fled away,* and all the lost face individual judgment on the basis of their works (verse 13).

None of the saved are here; it is not a question of salvation now – those who appear here are already damned. The question is degree of punishment commensurate with the responsibility of the individual.

Luke 12:47, 48, strongly suggests that responsibility will be determined not only by what a person did but by what he knew. *To him that knoweth to do good, and doeth it not, to him it is sin* (James 4:17).

Notice that the second resurrection takes place here (Revelation 20:12 - 15). Death and Hell signify the division of soul and body. The body comes from the grave, the place of death, and the soul comes from Hell, the depository of lost souls. Resurrected, they are judged and cast into the Lake of Fire where they suffer body, soul, and spirit forever.

REMEDY
There has never been any permanent remedy for man's ills. Man himself is incurable. He must become a new creation through the new birth before he can begin to overcome that depraved nature which is his by birth. The earth and heaven itself now become new. They are a new creation for new creatures - a prepared place for a prepared people. The seven great tests are over. The trial is finished, the verdict is in, and the sentence is executed.

God now brings the final remedy
> *And I saw a new heaven and a new earth: for the first heaven and the first earth were passed away; and there was no more sea. And I John saw the holy city, new Jerusalem, coming down from God out of heaven, prepared as a bride adorned for her husband. And I heard a great voice out of heaven saying, Behold, the tabernacle of God is with men, and he will dwell with them, and they shall be his people, and God himself shall be with them, and be their God* (Revelation 21:1 – 3).

The study of the seven dispensations of God's dealing with man have taken us from Paradise to Paradise – Paradise lost, to Paradise regained. History, is indeed, His Story. The puzzle has a "Big Picture" and God has allowed us to see how the pieces fit together. We are looking at the whole elephant, not just groping about his leg or tail.

What every generation needs, and this generation is no exception, is a metanarrative – a story that gives meaning to history, to life and to each individual. We need a story that can tell us where we came from, why we are here, who we are and where we are going.

I believe a study of the dispensations of Scripture can do that better than anything else and so I recommend it to a generation adrift in Postmodern doubt. May God be pleased to use it.

In the final section I want to address a number of issues and questions that may have been raised by a study like this and attempt to show that there is a Scriptural answer to those questions. I also want to show how understanding the dispensations and factoring in what we have learned, can help us *rightly divide* (correctly interpret) some of the more difficult passages of Scripture. I believe you may find this next section particularly exciting and helpful.

SECTION THREE:
ADDITIONAL ISSUES AND CONSIDERATIONS

CHAPTER SIXTEEN: MAKING DISPENSATIONAL DISTINCTIONS

When Paul exhorted Timothy to *Rightly Divide the Word of Truth*, he was literally telling him to "cut a straight line" separating those things which differ. The Apostle counted it a sign of maturity to be able to make distinctions, to be able to distinguish things that differ. Both the Old Testament and New exhort God's people to have discernment.

> *But strong meat belongeth to them that are of full age, even those who by reason of use have their senses exercised to discern both good and evil* (Hebrews 5:14).

> *And they shall teach my people the difference between the holy and profane, and cause them to discern between the unclean and the clean* (Ezekiel 44:23).

> *He answered and said unto them, When it is evening, ye say, It will be fair weather: for the sky is red. And in the morning, It will be foul weather to day: for the sky is red and lowring. O ye hypocrites, ye can discern the face of the sky; but can ye not discern the signs of the times* (Matthew 16:2, 3)?

Ironically, this is exactly where one of the major attacks is leveled at Dispensationalists. According to some, we are too discerning – we have made too many distinctions. The new anti-Dispensationalism accuses Dispensationalists of dualism for making distinctions between Israel and the Church, the Old Nature and the New Nature (a doctrine particularly under fire just now), the two resurrections, etc. But it is exactly those "distinctions" which allow the believer to make sense of Scripture.

Nothing helped the saints of the past several generations in their understanding of Scripture and walk with God more than C. I. Scofield's little booklet, *Rightly Dividing the Word of Truth*. Like all human efforts, one can find fault with certain statements which, if Scofield were alive today, he probably would not have made.

But the facts are indisputable – There is a difference between **The Jew, the Gentile, and the Church of God, The Two Advents of Christ, The Two Resurrections, (one to life and the other to eternal death), Law and Grace, The Believer's Two Natures, The Believer's Standing and State, Salvation and Rewards and Believers and Pretenders.** When we make those distinctions, we take the confusion out of Bible study. Contrary wise, when those distinctions are not made, confusion is created and the Scriptures seem to contradict themselves.

I recently read two commentaries by good men who would not hesitate to affirm that salvation is a free gift received by faith and bestowed by nothing else than the unmerited favor of God. Nevertheless, in interpreting a passage regarding the believer's rewards, they did so in a way that made salvation itself appear to be the result of human effort.

Salvation is a gift – rewards are earned. When those distinctions are not kept clearly in mind, not only can it lead to confusion, but it is the doorway to false doctrine. The Dispensationalist is not just talking about dispensational distinctions when he insists on *rightly dividing the Word of Truth* – he is talking about all kind of distinctions that must be made if we are to teach the truth.

Some of my dearest friends insist that there has ever only been "one gospel – the gospel of Grace." Yet when Jesus and the disciples preached *the Gospel of the Kingdom*, its content and focus was on the promises made to the nation Israel throughout the Old Testament Scriptures. It announced that the King was present and the Kingdom was about to be inaugurated.

It was completely different in content from Paul's gospel which he defined as, *Christ died for our sins according to the scriptures; and that he was buried, and that he rose again the third day according to the scriptures;. . ."* (1 Corinthians 15:3, 4).

It was also different from what John calls, *The Everlasting Gospel* whose message is *Fear God, and give glory to him; for the hour of his judgment is come: and worship him that made heaven, and earth, and the sea, and the fountains of waters* (Revelation 14:7).

If you are willing to allow the text to speak for itself, you must distinguish the difference between the subjects and content of those proclamations. Each of them was referred to as the **euaggelion** *(Good News -- Gospel)*, but each is news of a different kind, at a different time, to a different group of people.

Another crucial area of distinction is in the matter of the Judgments of Scripture. Will there really be just one great general judgment in which all will be judged? If so, is that where we finally find out our destiny either to heaven or to hell? – and if that is true, how can we have assurance of salvation now?

If we are willing to bow before the text we cannot help but discern that the judgments of Scripture occur at different times, in different places, with different people and for different purposes. In fact, the only thing those judgments have in common is the Judge.

It is this kind of careful distinction which Dispensationalists urge and which is being largely rejected by a newer breed of Bible expositor. Dr. David Larsen described it well when he wrote, "In our times we have the "new Hermeneutic" and literary deconstruction with its move away from the author [i.e., what the writer said], to reader-response [i.e., what the reader understood]. <u>Normative interpretation of the text is jettisoned in favor of whatever the reader would make of it.</u>" [1]

We dare not allow ourselves to be drawn back into the cloudy abyss of failing to ask the necessary and crucial questions of the text. Who said it? To whom was it addressed? To what period of time is it referring? Is the statement or promise for this time and dispensation or for another past or future time?

The present growing state of confusion in what calls itself evangelicalism is largely due to this failure to discern, discriminate, and demand that the text be allowed to say what it means and address those it addresses. This generation is deeply in need of a remedial course in *Rightly Dividing the Word of Truth*.

CHAPTER SEVENTEEN:
SALVATION IN DISPENSATIONALISM

One of the misunderstandings (or deliberate misrepresentations) of Dispensationalism is that is teaches different ways of salvation in the different dispensations. This charge has been addressed often enough and with enough clarity that to continue to perpetuate it is simply dishonest – but because that dishonesty persists we will address it once again.

Biblical Ministries Worldwide (BMW) is a mission that clearly espouses a Dispensational understanding of Scripture. But they clearly address this matter in their doctrinal statement which reads in part:

> "We believe the Scriptures interpreted in their natural, literal sense reveal divinely determined dispensations, which define man's responsibility in successive ages. A dispensation is not a way of salvation, but a divinely-ordered stewardship by which God directs man according to His purpose. *(John 1:17; 1 Corinthians 9:17; 2 Corinthians 3:9-18; Galatians 3:13-25; Ephesians 1:10; 3:2-10; Colossians 1:24-25; Hebrews 7:19; Revelation 20:2-6)*"

> "There are some who claim that Dispensationalism teaches that God changes the way of salvation and that is, or course, false and must never be implied. BMW clarifies this in the following; "We believe salvation is always by grace through faith regardless of the dispensation in which the believer may have lived. God's purpose of salvation by grace through faith alone has always been based upon the substitutionary atonement of our Lord Jesus Christ upon the cross. *(Ephesians 2:8-10; Hebrews 11:6; 1 Peter 1:10-12"* 1

The source of this contention is the belief held by our reformed brethren that not only was salvation always by grace through faith, but that faith always focused upon **the same content**, that is the death, burial and resurrection of the God-Man. In considering this matter therefore, we must address the question of what was the exact content of the faith that saved in the Old Testament period.

Distinction must be made between man's salvation in any given dispensation and his Dispensational Responsibility. Man's salvation always results from faith, made possible by grace and involves believing God and what God has said. Dispensational Responsibility results from God's progressive revelation of Himself and His plans.

Hence, under the Dispensation of Conscience, faith was expressed by offering the sacrifice for sin which God had instructed. God called Abel's offering, *a more excellent sacrifice* and specifically tells us that it was offered *by faith* (Hebrews 11:4).

God had clearly demonstrated to Adam and Eve the "blood offering" when He clothed them in coats of skin to cover their nakedness. The guilty pair were painfully aware of their physical nakedness, but God was more aware of their spiritual nakedness and that they had nothing that could adequately cover that nakedness or remove the guilt of sin. Whatever Adam an Eve might have understood from the lesson of that first blood sacrifice, this much is clear, they knew that they were now covered and that blood had been shed to make that possible.

Dispensationalists generally believe in progressive revelation both in the Old and the New Testaments. That means that the full revelation of many doctrines, revealed to us through the New Testament Epistles, was not revealed to the saints of former Dispensations. Through the lens of New Testament truth, we may extract the entire redemption plan out of the words, *And I will put enmity between thee and the woman, and between thy seed and her seed; it shall bruise thy head, and thou shalt bruise his heel* (Genesis 3:15), but I very much doubt that Eve could do that.

Preeminent among those doctrines anticipated in the Old Testament but fully revealed in the New was that of God's atoning sacrifice through the death of the God-man. While it is true that John the Baptizer announced, *Behold the Lamb of God that taketh away the sin of the world* (John 1:29), and Caiaphas the High Priest prophesied, *it is expedient for us, that one man should die for the people, and that the whole nation perish not* (John 11:50), even those statements do not show that there was any complete understanding of what would be involved in the death and resurrection of God's Son for our redemption. After all, was it not the same John who later sent his disciples asking, *Art thou he that should come, or look we for another* (Luke 7:19)?

It was Peter, who a moment after he had made the most powerful declaration ever uttered of that truth upon which the Church itself would later be built – *Thou art the Christ, the Son of the Living God* (Matthew 16:16), upon hearing Christ testify of His coming death, *began to rebuke him,* saying, *Be it far from thee, Lord; this shall not be unto thee* (16:22). The disciples clearly did not understand at that time the content of the gospel they would later preach.

Jesus Himself revealed clearly the substitutional nature of His atonement when he, *took bread, and blessed it, and brake it, and gave it to the disciples, and said, Take, eat; this is my body. And he took the cup, and gave thanks, and gave it to them, saying, Drink ye all of it; For this is my blood of the new testament, which is shed for many for the remission of sins* (Matthew 26:26 – 28). But their subsequent actions did not convey that even after that they understood what He was saying.

The truth is that Jesus' very own disciples, those who had walked with Him and whom He had taught for three years, never understood any of it until after Christ had died and was risen again. It was only then, that, *beginning at Moses and all the prophets, he expounded unto them in all the scriptures the things concerning himself.* (Luke 24:27). It was only after the resurrection that it is written, *Then opened he their understanding, that they might understand the scriptures* (Luke 24:45).

With the knowledge imparted through the Epistles, we read the Old Testament Scriptures and see Christ and His atoning sacrifice revealed in word and symbol throughout. But if we were to read those same passages without the benefit of that New Testament revelation, most of us would be no better off than the Ethiopian who, reading from Isaiah chapter fifty three, (one of the clearest passages in Scripture concerning the atoning work of Christ), asked, *of whom speaketh the prophet this – of himself, or of some other man* (Acts 8:34)?

Consider the message preached throughout the transitional book of Acts. As you read through the preaching in Acts, you will fail to find mention of a "substitutionary atonement" or any clear explanation of the ground upon which God can remain just and holy and yet forgive sin.

The exact basis for that forgiveness is nowhere clearly defined until Paul writes,

> *But now the righteousness of God without the law is manifested, being witnessed by the law and the prophets; Even the righteousness of God which is by faith of Jesus Christ unto all and upon all them that believe: for there is no difference: For all have sinned, and come short of the glory of God; Being*

> *justified freely by his grace through the redemption that is in Christ Jesus: Whom God hath set forth to be a propitiation through faith in his blood, to declare his righteousness for the remission of sins that are past, through the forbearance of God; To declare, I say, at this time his righteousness: that he might be just, and the justifier of him which believeth in Jesus* (Romans 3:21 – 26).

Ah, there it is – that is how God can freely and graciously forgive and how He graciously and freely forgave Old Testament saints. He can do so because Christ is made *a propitiation* (literally a satisfaction), for all sin, past and future, and God has accepted that perfect and sufficient payment.

Now it all comes together and we see the Divine plan, and looking back we can see it throughout all of Scripture. We understand what was witnessed by the Law and the prophets because we have the completed revelation clearly before us. But on what basis do we assume that the saints of the Old Testament were endowed with the same content of faith?

Peter indicates that the prophets themselves often struggled to understand the things they were writing, specifically when it concerned the mystery of the atonement:

> *Of which salvation the prophets have enquired and searched diligently, who prophesied of the grace that should come unto you: Searching what, or what manner of time the Spirit of Christ which was in them did signify, when it testified beforehand the sufferings of Christ, and the glory that should follow. Unto whom it was revealed, that not unto themselves, but unto us they did minister the things, which are now reported unto you by them that have preached the gospel unto you with the Holy Ghost sent down from heaven; which things the angels desire to look into* (1 Peter 1:10 – 12).

So now we must honestly ask ourselves the question, how much of that do you suppose Adam understood as he looked down at the covering of skin that now hid his nakedness? Or did Abel fully understand all that when he offered his *more excellent sacrifice?* Or even Abraham when he offered up Isaac on the very hill where it was said, *God will provide himself a lamb for a burnt offering* (Genesis 22:8). Perhaps he came closer than any other when he, *called the name of that place Jehovah Jireh: as it is said to this day, In the mount of the LORD it shall be seen.* (Genesis 22:14).

It is easy for us to read the New Testament revelation of the atonement back into the Old Testament record. It is easy for us to say that we are saved by looking backward to the Cross while they were saved by looking forward to it.

Well, maybe, but probably it would be more accurate to say, "We are saved by trusting God's promise to us, *Believe on the Lord Jesus Christ and thou shalt be saved,* because God looks at the Cross of His Son and is satisfied (propitiated), and they were saved by trusting God's promise to them (whatever the specific promise might have been), because God looked forward to the Cross of His Son and was satisfied.

If it was so difficult for even Christ's own Disciples to grasp the full meaning of the birth and death and resurrection of the Son of God, how much was the substitutionary death of the Son of God comprehended by the saints of the Old Testament – or was the focus of their faith God Himself and His word as in each individual case, they obeyed the revelation they had. I personally believe it was clearly that.

In Paul's great discussion of Justification by faith found in Romans chapter four he says, *what saith the scripture? Abraham believed God, and it was counted unto him for righteousness* (Romans 4:3). What did he believe? He believed God's promise that he would have a seed as numerous as the stars in heaven.

Later in the same chapter Paul specifically sets the time when Abraham was justified by his faith. It was before circumcision, before the formal ratifying of the covenant (see: Genesis 15:9 – 21), simply on the verbal promise of God.

This same pattern can be seen throughout the eleventh chapter of Hebrews. What did Abel believe? He believed that if he would offer a blood sacrifice as his father, Adam, had taught him, God would accept that sacrifice and put away his sins (see Hebrews 9:15). Enoch believed God and walked in fellowship with Him. Noah believed God's testimony and built an ark. Abraham believed God concerning a seed and a Land. Joseph believed God concerning the promise of deliverance from Egypt (Hebrews 11:22), and Rahab believed that Israel's God was a true and living God and risked her life to save the spies.

In each case <u>the specific content of their faith</u> was not the thing that was important, but the object of their faith – they believed God! Hence the pattern of faith throughout the Old Testament is seen to be a faith in the testimony of God which results in acting upon that testimony.

It is true that there were those exceptional individuals who seemed to grasp that God's redemption would be through Messiah, as seen in Simeon and Anna (Luke 2:25 – 38), but they are few and far between. The faith pattern up until the full revelation given in the New Testament was simply believing God and acting upon whatever revelation they had. Thus salvation in every dispensation is by grace through faith, and that faith is made perfect in the final atonement of Christ which was shed not only for our sins but, *for the remission of sins that are past through the forbearance of God* (Romans 3:25), and for *the transgressions that were under the first testament* (Hebrews 9:15).

So how does Dispensational testing that gives man different Responsibilities and adjusts his method of approaching God (Relationship) apply to this question? The Theological meaning of Dispensation is always a "stewardship or responsibility for a certain thing during a particular period of time."

Obviously, the Responsibility of the Dispensation of Conscience (to do well), was not a way to salvation, nor did exercising governmental authority to the glory of God in the next Dispensation constitute any salvific merit. The Dispensation of Promise deals primarily with the Land of Palestine and even the Dispensation of Law constituted, not a path to salvation, but a clear revelation of man's guilt and condemnation as Moses himself made clear in the words: *Cursed be he that confirmeth not all the words of this law to do them* (Deuteronomy 27:26).

As we have seen then, through each and all of these Dispensations, the way of salvation was faith in God and what God had said. Salvation was by grace through faith and the object of that faith was God Himself and His divine testimony. There is one Dispensation in which that pattern actually merges with man's Responsibility itself and that is the current Dispensation of Grace.

In the Dispensation of Grace the entire issue is now that Christ has offered Himself and atonement has been made, the test of this period is believing the gospel of God's grace and trusting Christ alone for salvation. All of the progressive revelation of the past has now fully flowered in the garden of divine grace and salvation through faith alone is the central Responsibility of this Dispensation. In this Dispensation and this alone, the Divine test (to believe the gospel) and the way of salvation are the same.

Perhaps it is that fact which might have confused some, but hopefully, what we have said will clarify our position. Salvation is always, and in every Dispensation made available by grace and received through faith, and the object of that faith is always God Himself and His Divine testimony.

The content of that testimony was not fully developed in former dispensations as it is today, but God passed by sins under the former economies and justified those who placed their faith in Him. He can now *declare His* (Christ's) *righteousness for the remission of the sin that are past* (Romans 3:26), through the propitiation which has been now provided in Christ's sacrifice.

CHAPTER EIGHTEEN:
DISPENSATIONAL PERSPICUITY

One of the hallmarks of the Reformation was the insistence on the part of the Reformers in what was called, "the perspicuity of Scripture." Webster defines perspicuity as "something that can be seen through, i.e., lucidity, clearness of style or exposition, freedom from obscurity." [1]

The issue of perspicuity came to the fore as early reformers attempted to give the Bible to the common people in their own language. The Roman Catholic Church fought adamantly against this principle. To Rome, giving the common man the Bible to read would lead to the common man interpreting what he read. In Rome's thinking, only the Magisterium (or the teaching office) of the Church had the right and authority to interpret Scripture. The Roman Catholic Church asserts that Scripture is imperspicuous (unclear) apart from the interpretative framework of the Catholic Church and tradition.

The reformers, Wycliffe, Huss, Luther and Calvin all argued that the Bible was clear when it came to its essential message. Contrary to the dominant Roman Catholic idea which said that the Bible was difficult and obscure, Protestants said that anyone who was literate and diligent could comprehend the gospel and the Scriptures.

"The Reformers did not say that all of Scripture was equally understandable or even that scholarly study wasn't necessary. What they did say was that the essential clarity of the Word of God was self-evident. Responsible interpretation of the Bible by those in the pews was not only to be expected, but also to be encouraged. God's Word was never intended to be esoteric, dark, enigmatic, cryptic, abstruse, obscure, ambiguous, occluded, enshrouded, inscrutable, or vague. Rather, it is a perfect, sure, right, pure, clean and true light, illuminating the character and plan of God." 2

Consider the following Scripture:

> *Your word is a lamp to my feet, and a light to my path* (Psalm 119:105).

> *The entrance of thy words giveth light; it giveth understanding unto the simple* (Psalm 119:130 KJV).

Or consider it in the Contemporary English Version (CEV) *Understanding your word brings light to the minds of ordinary people* (Psalm 119:130 CEV). It would appear that God intended his Word to be read and understood by every man.

What has perspicuity of Scripture to do with Dispensationalism? The answer, I believe, is that both share this same characteristic. That is to say that a dispensational approach to Scripture is not, "esoteric, dark, enigmatic, cryptic, abstruse, obscure, ambiguous, occluded, enshrouded, inscrutable, or vague."

In contrast to that inscrutable method which views all of the Bible's message as fitting into three (or perhaps two) "implied" covenants which are never stated in Scripture but only assumed, and which confounds sage and saint alike, Dispensationalism approaches Scripture by accepting a very clear, plain and literal understanding of the biblical text. The covenants which form the framework of its system are not contrived or "theological" in nature, but biblical and plainly set forth within the pages of Scripture.

Even the simplest reader can read those covenants in the pages of Scripture and grasp the idea of the biblical covenants governing history. He can further grasp the idea of progressive revelation leading to progressive periods of testing. It can be plainly seen by anyone that man's condition in Eden in his innocent state, varied drastically from his condition after his transgression. And when a consistent hermeneutic of Historical-Grammatical interpretation is used, the distinctions in Scripture become evident.

That is one of the reasons Dispensationalism caught on so quickly and spread so rapidly both in Europe and America. Suddenly, the common man in the pew could understand God's big story. The theology of things to come was no longer the exclusive possession of the clergy or the seminaries.

The result was a proliferation of Bible conferences, Bible teaching radio programs, Bible institutes, faith mission societies, and even new denominations and fellowships all firmly committed to a Dispensational approach to Scripture.

Bible classes sprang up in many churches and even beyond the Church in homes and public venues. Dispensational Charts gave the truth a visual dimension and made the outlines of Scripture plain. Clarence Larkin, H. A. Ironside and others developed visual charts that defined the distinctions between Israel and the Church, the Resurrections, the Judgments and a host of other crucial subjects. Many felt that for the first time, they were beginning to understand and grasp the teaching of Scripture on these subjects.

Dr. Donald G. Barnhouse's little book, *Teaching the Word of Truth* patterned itself after C. I. Scofield's earlier booklet, *Rightly Dividing The Word of Truth*. Both set forth the same biblical distinctions between Israel and the Church, The Old Nature and The New, The Believer's Standing and State, Faith and Works, Salvation and Rewards, and the Dispensational Periods of Testing.

It was the dispensational teaching of men like Charles E. Fuller, Dr. M. R. DeHaan, and Dr. Theodore Epp that first made the Scriptures understandable to me. As a young man, newly saved, I spent hours, far into the night, studying and reading everything I could get from Radio Bible Class, Back to the Bible and my Scofield Reference Bible.

Coming from an old-line denominational church where Bible stories were used to make moral applications but never to present a comprehensive understanding of what God was doing in the world, Dispensationalism provided me with both the big picture overview of Scripture and the details to make up that picture. The systematic theology of Dispensationaism opened the Bible to me as never before.

I have found in my ministry, both in the United States and abroad that Dispensational teaching always has the same effect. I taught Dispensational truth as a young pastor in my first Church to my adult Sunday School class and watched the class take on a completely new dynamic. For the first time, my people got excited about the Word of God.

Whether I am teaching through two interpreters, using three languages to an indigenous tribe, or speaking to a college educated audience in a major city, teaching through the dispensations brings an excited response from listeners. And why not? If you take the Word of God for what it says and allow it to speak for itself, it is remarkable how perspicuous Scripture becomes.

Dispensationalists speak often about literal interpretation; although I prefer the more graphic phrase, historical-grammatical literal interpretation. I have been challenged by some who claim it is difficult or maybe even impossible to distinguish between that which is literal and that which is symbolic. I think that is a gross overstatement and misunderstanding. In most cases the distinction is actually quite simple.

When I read, *The trees of the field shall clap their hands* (Isaiah 55:12), I know I am reading words which are figurative. However, I also know that the figure has a literal meaning and that God is using a poetic description to inform me that all creation will rejoice at His appearing. *The creation itself also shall be delivered from the bondage of corruption into the glorious liberty of the children of God* (Romans 8:21 MKJV). Now how really difficult is that?

But, when I read a forthright statement such as, *The Lord God shall give unto Him the throne of His father David and He shall reign over the house of Jacob forever, and of His Kingdom there shall be no end* (Luke 1:32, 33), I have no difficulty understanding that God means exactly what He said. *"Jesus shall reign, where'er the sun, doth its successive journeys run, His Kingdom stretched from shore to shore, till moon shall wax and wane no more."*

Literal interpretation simply means taking the words of Scripture in the plain ordinary sense in which you would understand them in any other form of literature. And if a passage of Scripture seems less than perspicuous, remember that Scripture is its own best commentary. If you search, you will find the explanation to the obscure text within Scripture itself.

The perspicuity of Scripture made it available to the common man bringing about the greatest spiritual awakening the world ever experienced. The perspicuity of the dispensational approach to Scripture, based upon a clear historical-grammatical literal interpretation, allowed the common people to distinguish the ages and discern the movement of God across the pages of biblical history. That understanding in turn produced an army of men and women who valued, studied, understood and propagated the Word of God like nothing that had ever happened before.

George E. Ladd, a harsh critic of Dispensationalism, confesses concerning this movement that:

> "It is doubtful if there has been any other circle of men who have done more by their influence in preaching, teaching and writing to promote a love for Bible study, a hunger for the deeper Christian life, a passion for evangelism and zeal for missions in the history of American Christianity." [3]

If I have said it before, forgive me, but if the fruit is good, the tree that produced it is good. The fruit of Dispensationalism has been extraordinarily good as even it opponents recognize.

CHAPTER NINETEEN: DISPENSATIONAL vs. COVENANT THEOLOGY

"Covenant theology is a Calvinist interpretive framework for understanding the overall message of the Bible. It uses the theological concept of "covenant" as an organizing principle for Christian theology. The standard description of covenant theology views the history of God's dealings with mankind, from Creation to the Fall, to Redemption, to Consummation, under the framework of two or three overarching theological covenants." 1

If two covenants are assumed, then they are the "Covenant of Works" and the "Covenant of Grace." If the theologian assumes three covenants, the "Covenant of Redemption" is added.

Gary Gilley writes of these:

> **The Covenant of Works which was between God and Adam**: This is seen as an agreement between God and Adam promising life to Adam for perfect obedience and promising death as the penalty for failure. Adam sinned and thus man failed to meet the requirements of the Covenant of Works. Michael Horton, a strong advocate of Covenant Theology, admits that the Covenant of Works

cannot be found explicitly in Scripture but believes it is implied in the creation narrative.

The Covenant of Grace between God and sinful mankind: As a result of man's failure, a second covenant became necessary. This is viewed as the gracious agreement between the offended God and the offending, but elect sinner, in which God promises salvation through faith in Christ, and the sinner accepts this promise by faith.

The Covenant of Redemption which was an agreement between the Father and Son is held by some but not all covenantalists. O. Palmer Robertson challenges this covenant on the basis of exegesis. He writes, "Scripture simply does not say much on the pre-creation shape of the decrees of God. [To speak of such] is to extend the bounds of scriptural evidence beyond propriety." Nevertheless this is believed by some to be an agreement between the Father and the Son in which the Father gives His Son as the Redeemer of the elect, and the Son voluntarily takes the place for those elect whom the Father had given Him. 2

These covenants (whether two or three) are called "theological covenants" because they are not explicitly named or identified in the Bible. Rather, they are thought to be theologically implicit, that is, implied by the narrative, and Covenant Theologians believe that they describe and summarize Scriptural data.

Within historical Reformed systems of thought, covenant theology is not merely treated as a point of doctrine or a central dogma, but the very structure by which the biblical text organizes itself and through which it must be interpreted.

As a framework for biblical interpretation, covenant theology stands in contrast to Dispensationalism which bases its framework of interpretation upon a literal/historical/grammatical interpretation of the actual Biblical covenants, that is, those explicitly defined in the text of Scripture.

The Scofield Reference Bible lists eight covenants: (1) the Edenic Covenant: Genesis 1:28 – 30; and (2) the Adamic Covenant: Genesis 3:14 – 19, (3) the Noahic Covenant Genesis 8:20 – 22; 9:9 – 17; (4) the Abrahamic Covenant Genesis 12:1-3; 13:14-18; 15:1-21; 17:1-22; 22:15-18; and also reaffirmed to Isaac, Genesis 26:2 – 5; and later to Jacob, Genesis 28:12 – 15; and finally to all his posterity, Psalms 105:9 – 12; (5) the Mosaic Covenant: Exodus 19, 20; (6) the Palestinian Covenant: Deuteronomy 29, 30; (7) the Davidic Covenant: 2 Samuel 7:8 – 16; and (8) the New Covenant: Jeremiah 31:31 – 37. [3]

While many Dispensationalists accept all of the eight covenants enumerated by Dr. C. I. Scofield in the Scofield Reference Bible, the fact is that the first two, the so-called Edenic Covenant, and the Adamic Covenant are not called covenants in Scripture. The first time the word covenant appears is in Genesis six where God establishes His covenant with Noah to deliver him from the flood. The Noahic Covenant is later expanded by God to assure mankind that there will never be another global flood (Genesis 9:8 – 17).

Of the other six covenants, the Mosaic Covenant was declared to be temporary, (*added because of transgressions <u>until</u> the Seed should come;* [Galatians 3:19]). The others are all eschatological in that they promise things which have not yet been completely fulfilled. There is a lengthy and detailed discussion of each of the eschatological covenants in my earlier book, ***The Prophetic Destiny of Israel & the Islamic Nations***.

Covenant theology is also referred to as "supersessionism," or "replacement theology," due to the fact that it teaches that the Church has superseded national Israel and will "spiritually fulfill" the promises of the actual Biblical covenants. Once again I quote Gary Gilley:

"The covenantal system has many implications, not the least of which is that it recognizes no discontinuity between Israel and the church. That is, the promises to the nation of Israel, found especially in the Old Testament, are now being fulfilled in spiritual form in the church which is spiritual Israel. Physical and land promises yet to be fulfilled by Israel are either renounced because of Israel's rebelliousness or have been fulfilled symbolically. In the Old Testament Israel was the church, in the New Testament the church is comprised of both Jews and Gentiles. No future remains for the nation of Israel in the program of God. This interpretation is made possible because covenantal theologians, who faithfully employ historical-grammatical hermeneutics throughout most of Scripture employ an allegorical/symbolic hermeneutic especially involving the future prophetic portions of the Bible. Covenantalists see most prophecies as already fulfilled allegorically or symbolically and the church is the recipient of the Old Testament covenant promises to Israel. Most also equate the church with the kingdom of God and believe we are presently in the kingdom, at least in its initial stage." [4]

There is a technical point that needs to be made here. Covenant Theologians do not, as is sometimes charged, teach that God has abandoned the promises made to the Jews and has replaced the Jews with Christians as His chosen people in the earth. Rather, Covenant theologians say that they; "see the fulfillment of the promises to Israel in the person and the work of the Messiah, Jesus of Nazareth, who established the church in organic continuity with Israel, not a separate replacement entity." [5]

In other words, Covenant Theology sees the Church as a mere spiritual of Israel. Since Israel rejected and crucified their Messiah, God no longer has any "earthly" people, but only a heavenly people made up of all the saved of the ages beginning with Adam.

Covenant Theologians reach this conclusion by applying the logic of the so-called Covenant of Grace, or Covenants of Grace and Redemption as the over-arching principles of history. Hence the entire story of the Bible is a story of the spiritual redemption of mankind and nothing more.

When expressed within the context of Covenant Theological assumptions, the conclusion may appear sound. But please notice that in order to reach this conclusion, at least two assumptions must be made. First, we must assume the validity of the Theological covenants of works and of grace. But these "covenants" are nowhere mentioned in Scripture, and there is not clear agreement on them even among Covenant theologians.

Westminster Confession of Faith, teaches that the Mosaic covenant was fundamentally an administration of the over-arching Covenant of Grace. On the other hand, Meredith G. Kline, building on prior work by George E. Mendenhall, argued that comparisons between the suzerainty-vassal treaties and royal grants of the Ancient Near East provide insight in highlighting certain distinctive features of the Mosaic covenant as a law covenant. [5] There is much scholarly work among covenant theologians but no agreement on the details of these assumed covenants.

The second assumption that must be made is that prophetic Scripture, which seems to clearly promise a future for Israel as a national entity, must be understood and interpreted in a "spiritual sense," and is therefore fulfilled, or will be fulfilled by the Church. Hence, words such as *Zion* must be made to refer, not to a literal earthly place within the walls of Jerusalem, but to heaven. As the hymn writer expresses it, we are, "*Marching upward to Zion, the beautiful city of God.*" All this illustrates the fact again, that he who defines the words controls the argument.

Covenant Theology is a logical system if we accept the combined premises of the existence of two (or three) over-arching theologically assumed covenants that define both the past and the future Biblically, and if we are willing to adapt a non-literal, non-historical, and non-grammatical hermeneutic when we approach passages that seem to clearly predict a future for national Israel.

It is exactly at these two points that the Dispensational and Covenant Theologian part company. First, the Dispensationalist sees no demonstrable evidence of the assumed theological covenants which even the Covenant Theologians admit are nowhere stated.

It is all very nice to talk about God the Father establishing an agreement with God the Son for man's redemption, or and a covenant with Adam, but where do we find that in Scripture? Of course, we may perhaps argue from silence for such a "covenant"– but to force all of Scripture and history into a never declared theological construction seems shaky at the very least.

The second assumption is even more suspect. Where do we find the license to switch from a literal/historical/grammatical hermeneutic to a contrived "spiritualized" interpretation just in order to force the text to support the first assumption of these two or three over-arching theological covenants, which are themselves undeclared?

The real distinction between Dispensationalism and Reformed Theology is that the former makes every effort to rest its case upon the text itself. It is not a system imposed upon the Scripture, but one derived from it. It rests upon real historically recorded covenants, not theoretical ones. It embraces the literal/historical/grammatical reading of the Scripture and derives its teaching from that.

That is doubtless why so many laymen have found Dispensationalism attractive and satisfying. As one said, "I'm not philosophical enough to be a covenant theologian – that is why I am a dispensationalist. I just assume God means what He says."

The question is, did God really intend His Word to be understood only by the philosophically inclined, or did He intend us to take what He clearly says and rest our case upon it?

CHAPTER TWENTY:
THE CHURCH AGE
- A Prophetic Parenthesis

One of my favorite books in the early stages of my ministry was a small volume by H.A. Ironside entitled, *The Great Parenthesis*. In it, Ironside demonstrates that from the standpoint of Old Testament Prophecy, the Church Age can be compared to a parenthesis in a sentence.

God has a great deal to say throughout the Old Testament about Israel, her future and destiny, and about Messiah, both in His first Advent and His Second, but has absolutely nothing to say about the Church.

In fact, it is clear from Paul's word in Ephesians that keeping the "one Body, the Church" a secret was God's purpose and plan and that to unfold that Mystery, or secret, now reveals the "manifold wisdom of God."

> *Unto me, who am less than the least of all saints, is this grace given, that I should preach among the Gentiles the unsearchable riches of Christ; And to make all men see what is the fellowship of the mystery, which from the beginning of the world hath been hid in God, who created all things by*

> *Jesus Christ: To the intent that now unto the principalities and powers in heavenly places might be known by the church the manifold wisdom of God, According to the eternal purpose which he purposed in Christ Jesus our Lord* (Ephesian 3:8 – 11).

It is most interesting in this text that in the revelation of this *Mystery,* God's wisdom is not only revealed to us, but to the principalities and powers in the heavens. In other words, even the angelic hosts did not suspect that through Israel's rejection of both Messiah, and the Messianic Kingdom, their terrible error would open the door for God to begin a brand new work with an Assembly from every kindred, tribe and nation which He calls the Church.

God's "Time Clock" of prophecy is found in Daniel chapter nine, specifically in verses twenty four through twenty seven. No one has successfully been able to challenge the careful work done by Sir Robert Anderson in his classic book, *The Coming Prince.* In it he traces the smallest details of Daniel's prophecy and sets precisely the exact time when the prophetic "Time clock" started.

Daniel had been told that, *from the going forth of the commandment to restore and to build Jerusalem unto the Messiah the Prince shall be seven weeks, and threescore and two weeks* (Daniel 9:25). Anderson's first task was to understand and demonstrate the meaning of the Hebrew word shabua translated *week.* Was it to be understood to mean a week of seven days, as we would generally understand it, or something quite different? For this discussion, I will borrow generously from my preceding book, ***The Future Destiny of Israel & The Islamic Nations***, in which I discussed this particular prophecy.

> "God told Daniel that seventy weeks or *shabua* (a Hebrew word that simply means "a seven") were determined upon his people Israel. It quickly becomes obvious upon closer scrutiny that Daniel was not to understand mere periods of seven days, but rather seventy sets of seven

years. Hence the entire period of time God set to finish His testing of Israel would be 490 years." 1

Now the next hurdle for understanding the prophecy was to determine the exact starting point indicated by the text: *from the going forth of the commandment to restore and to build Jerusalem* (Daniel 9:25). Remember, Jerusalem had been destroyed in 586 B.C. and if there was a decree for its rebuilding, what decree was it and when was it issued? Answering those two questions was absolutely essential to understanding the prophecy.

Sir. Robert Anderson proves conclusively that the decree referred to in the prophecy was not the well known one issued by King Cyrus for the rebuilding of the Temple (Ezra 1:1 – 4), but rather, the decree issued by Artaxerxes to Nehemiah (see Nehemiah 2:1 – 8), for the express purpose of allowing the city of Jerusalem to be rebuilt.

In my former book, I mention that, "The historic date of that decree is one of the best established dates of history. It was March 14, 445 B.C. On that date, Artaxerxes issued a decree to Nehemiah (see Nehemiah 2:1 – 8), for the express purpose of allowing the city of Jerusalem to be rebuilt. The beginning of Daniel's time period then is dated from that decree." 2

Now let me explain why I expressed such strong confidence in that date. When attempting to determine the exact calendar date of the decree, Sir. Robert Anderson had requested assistance from the Royal Observatory located in Greenwich, England.

The Royal Observatory, played a major role in the history of astronomy and navigation, and is best known as the location of the prime meridian. It is situated on a hill in Greenwich Park, overlooking the River Thames, and its calculations are the gold standard of the world for determining time and navigation.

Sir. Robert Anderson included a copy of the response which he received from the Observatory concerning the question of when the decree of Artaxerxes was issued. Given the clear and precise date recorded by Nehemiah in the opening verse of chapter two, the Observatory had only to calculate the difference between the Jewish calendar and our own.

Daniel marks the beginning of the countdown at *the going forth of the commandment to restore and to build Jerusalem* which was given on March 14, 445 BC. (Notice that the time given by the Royal Observatory was Paris time, it being one day later in the Middle East).

Now we have established the first "bench mark" for computing the prophecy and I reproduce here their reply: 3

> " ROYAL OBSERVATORY, GREENWICH.
> " *June 26th,* 1877.
>
> " SIR,—I have had the moon's place calculated from Largeteau's Tables in Addition to the *Connaisance des Tons* 1846, by one of my assistants, and have no doubt of its correctness. The place being calculated for —444, March 12d. 2oh., French reckoning, or March 12d. 8h. P.M., it appears that the said time was short of New Moon by about 8h. 47m., and therefore the New Moon occurred at 4h. 47m. A.M., March 13th, Paris time.
> " I am, etc.,
> "(Signed,)G. B. AIRY."
>
> The new moon, therefore, occurred at Jerusalem on the 13th March, B.C. 445 (444 Astronomical) at 7h. 9m. A.M.

Daniel's prophetic calendar of 490 years was broken up into three time periods, seven weeks (49 years), three score and two weeks (62 x 7 or 434 years) and one final week (7 years). It is important to note the everywhere in Scripture, where time is broken up into days and months, Scripture is always dealing with literal days and months and each month always has exactly thirty days.

That fact is established as early as in the Flood account in

Genesis 7:11, and 8:3, 4. The period of the flood is stated as being five months and then as 150 days. The math is quite simple: 150 divided by 5 equals 30; hence five months of thirty days each.

Amazingly, when going to the final book of the New Testament, the book of Revelation, we find the same phenomena. Here the prophecy concerns the final three and one half years of Tribulation and it is variously referred to as 3 ½ years, 42 months, and 1260 days. Translation – each month has exactly thirty days.

Now please remember that Daniel's prophetic calendar of 490 years was broken up into the three time periods indicated previously. According to the prophecy, at the end of the first two periods, totaling 483 years, Daniel was told that Messiah the Prince would come, and indeed He did.

In exactly 483 prophetic years (173,880 days) which ended on April 6, 32 AD, Messiah Yeshua rode triumphantly into the city of Jerusalem on a day known to us as Palm Sunday, surrounded by the crowds crying, *Hosanna to the son of David*, a clear indication that they understood in this action that He was presenting Himself as King, just as Zechariah had prophesied: *Rejoice greatly, O daughter of Zion; shout, O daughter of Jerusalem: behold, thy King cometh unto thee: he is just, and having salvation; lowly, and riding upon an ass, and upon a colt the foal of an ass* (Zechariah 9:9).

It is the next part of the prophecy, however, that informs us concerning the subject at hand. Daniel was told that ***after*** the 483 years Messiah would be *cut off* or killed. Yeshua was crucified five days after his triumphal entry into the city (April 6, 32 AD).

Notice that Messiah's death did not happen during the 483 years. Daniel was distinctly told that is would be ***after*** and that becomes very clear in the Hebrew (אחר 'achar properly the *hind* part; generally used as an adverb or conjugation, *after* - or after that).

Hence we are not left to doubt. Messiah's death would not take place until after the sixty nine weeks of Daniel's prophetic calendar were ended – but it would take place <u>before</u> the beginning of the final seventieth week.

Notice the events which Daniel is told will transpire during that obvious interval between the sixty ninth and seventieth week of the prophecy. *And after threescore and two weeks shall Messiah be cut off, but not for himself: and the people of the prince that shall come shall destroy the city and the sanctuary; and the end thereof shall be with a flood, and unto the end of the war desolations are determined. And he shall confirm the covenant with many for one week:* (Daniel 9:26, 27).

Here we have listed the following events:

(1) Messiah's death (five days after the close of the 69 weeks),

(2) The destruction of the city of Jerusalem and the Temple Sanctuary (occurred 70 AD, thirty eight years after the close of the 69th week). Expositor, John Gill believes the "flood" signifies, "the number, power, and irresistible force of the enemy, and the sad devastation made by them:"[4] Albert Barnes concludes, "Flood,' appropriately denotes the ravages of an army, sweeping everything away. It would be like a sudden inundation, carrying everything before it. No one can doubt that this language is applicable in every respect to the desolations brought upon Jerusalem by the Roman armies." [5]

(3) *Desolations are determined* until the end of the conflict. Quite actually, the word "determined" bears the force of a decree. Until some unstated time in the future after her destruction, the sanctuary will lay desolate. As noted, the Temple was destroyed in 70 AD. How long would it be "until the end" – well, the temple mount is still destitute of the Temple and it has been thus destitute for over two thousand years.

The next calculation we have is the indication that this "Time Clock" will begin marking time again when a certain *covenant* is confirmed with the Jewish nation. Historically, that has not occurred, so we might say that from the standpoint of Daniel's Prophetic Calendar, we are now living in a vast period of time uncalculated by the prophecy. We are, if you please, in what could be described very properly as a "Parenthesis". Note, it is not a parenthesis in God's determinate plan, but a parenthesis in what God pleased to reveal, and therefore what we could know prophetically looking at Old Testament prophecy.

Right now, that indeterminate time, that parenthesis, has lasted over two thousand years. The entire Church Age, which had been kept a secret in the Old Testament, and which was never perceived by the prophets (Ephesians 3:5), is thus a parenthesis in Israel's prophetic calendar. Israel, prophetically speaking, cannot begin counting days again until that final seven year period begins.

That is what is meant therefore, when we speak of the Church Age as a "Parenthesis." We do not mean that it is in any way of lesser importance, but only that is was a secret kept by God and not revealed until our Lord first spoke of "building His Church." The very nature of the Church depended upon Christ's completed sacrifice and His victorious resurrection – therefore it could not have begun before those events.

Both of those events lay outside the prophetic time period designated by Daniel. Both occur "after" the 69th week, but before the 70th week. The Church has come into being and developed during this long undesignated interruption in Israel's prophetic calendar. Therefore, it is most descriptive to refer to it as, *The Great Parenthesis.*

Interestingly, this is the very point where Dispensationalism is most criticized by Anti-Dispensationalists. The Church of the New Testament is describes as Christ's Body and is composed of Jews as well as Gentiles. In it there is *neither Jew nor Greek, bond nor free, but all are one in Christ.*

It is a Body that is partaker of His own life through the Spirit, and whose destiny and rewards are heavenly in nature. It is a Body that never existed before the coming of the Holy Spirit at Pentecost, because it could not have. It is defined as: *By one Spirit are we all baptized into one body, whether we be Jews or Gentiles, whether we be bond or free, and have been all made to drink into one Spirit* (1 Corinthians 12:13). Since the Baptism of the Holy Spirit did not happen until Pentecost, the Body formed by that Baptism did not exist before that event.

In spite of what the Scripture says, and although there is not the least hint of that Church in the Old Testament, some still persist in believing that the Church began with Adam, or Abraham, thus their Doctrine of Ecclesiology (the Church) is quite different than that of the Dispensationalist.

Clarence Bass is one of those individuals and has written an entire book attempting to refute Dispensationalism and especially criticizing the concept of the Church Age as a "Parenthesis." [6]

Dr. David Larsen makes this telling reply:

> "Bass alleges that H.A. Ironside's use of the expression for the church age, "The Great Parenthesis" somehow means that "the church is parenthetical to God's ongoing purposes for mankind," some kind of an "interruption" in God's plan occasioned by Israel's rejection of their Messiah. Ironside has taken a lot of ridicule for this expression but it is curious that Bass does not footnote Ironsides' book on this subject. It is clear that the Church-age is parenthetic in the sense that it was not foreseen by the prophets of the Old Testament. That it was a "hidden interval" does not devalue or denigrate the extraordinary character and nature of what God has been doing among the nations through the world-wide propagation of the gospel message. [7]

No, the Church Age is only a Parenthesis in terms of God's program with Israel, but as the Scriptures clearly teach, it was a glorious secret known by God throughout the ages but now revealed through the Apostles, and such a marvelous plan, encompassing Jew and Gentile and every believing person, that the angelic hosts themselves marvel as they watch that plan unfold.

I believe the real reason behind this virulent reaction to the concept of the Church Age being parenthetical, is that if it is a parenthesis, then it necessarily implies something will follow it; and that something is nothing less that the oft prophesied future for National Israel, which is exactly what our non-dispensational friends will not accept.

CHAPTER TWENTY-ONE: DISPENSATIONAL TRANSITIONS

In the study of the dispensations, it is necessary, not only to observe the demarcation between one dispensation and another, but to understand that while God may have instituted something new, it often required a period of time for men to grasp what God was doing. If we look, we will find transitional periods occurring with each successive dispensation.

God instituted the Dispensation of Human Government with Noah soon after the flood. How long did it take for human government to become a reality and develop in its many forms? According to the genealogical table there were 952 years from Noah to Abraham. If we assume that the Tower of Babel incident occurred at the time of Peleg's birth (*for in his days was the earth divided*, [Genesis 10:25]), then we have at least 201 years from Noah to Peleg during which time human government gradually took form before it reached the rebellion of Babel. After that, we must presume that it continued to be developed in the many nations and people groups caused by the division of languages.

Another fact to remember is, that while a dispensational period may end, man's responsibility for the particular feature of that dispensation may not end. For instance, while the Dispensation of Conscience ended in man's failure and the judgment of the flood, man is still held accountable to live according to his conscience. Paul develops this in Romans 2:14 – 16; (*For when the Gentiles, which have not the law, do by nature the things contained in the law, these, having not the law, are a law unto themselves: Which show the work of the law written in their hearts, their conscience also bearing witness, and their thoughts the mean while accusing or else excusing one another); In the day when God shall judge the secrets of men by Jesus Christ according to my gospel.*

The dispensation therefore, tested the new responsibility, and demonstrated that man was not disposed to follow the moral instincts of the conscience God had given him. The dispensational test was over, but the moral obligation was not.

The same is true of the Dispensation of Human Government. While man failed in that period of testing, God still establishes human government and holds it accountable to act righteously. *Let every soul be subject unto the higher powers. For there is no power but of God: the powers that be are ordained of God.* (Romans 13:1). Governments are still ordained by God and rulers are called here *ministers of God* three times in six verses. The obligation of ruling for God is still upon human government.

One of the longest transitions occurs between the Dispensation of the Law and that of Grace. Remember, that while the Dispensation of Law was given distinctively to Israel, the Dispensation of Grace embraced all of humanity, and so there were a host of changes which had to take place. As this theme is developed in Scripture, the transition becomes most evident in the New Testament books of Matthew and Acts (which we will look at in greater detail in the next two chapters).

Matthew transitions us from the expected Kingdom for Israel, to the setting aside of that phase of the Kingdom and the description of how the Kingdom will develop in Mystery form (Matthew 13).

Acts carries that transition further, beginning with the question, *Lord, wilt thou at this time restore again the kingdom to Israel* (Acts 1:6)? Please note, that it is the prophesied earthly kingdom that they are still looking for. Jesus does not tell them that it will not come – only that they cannot know the timing of when it would come, and that at this moment there is another program at hand.

Acts proceeds through the repeated rejection of the gospel message by the Jews and their violent opposition (evident throughout the book), to Paul's final declaration in chapter twenty eight, *Be it known therefore unto you, that the salvation of God is sent unto the Gentiles, and that they will hear it* (Acts 28:28).

In the meantime, the Church itself struggles to define its new role as is manifest at the Jerusalem Council in Acts fifteen. Obviously, while the dispensation itself begins at the Cross, the full development of its character takes a period, that is measured in years to emerge, so that once again, we see a transitional period as we move from one dispensation to another.

I think it can be clearly stated that there is also a distinct transitional period between the close of the Dispensation of Grace and the beginning of the Dispensation of the Kingdom. Remember that the Dispensation of Grace must be distinguished from the Church Age. The Church Age occurs within the Dispensation of Grace.

The Dispensation of Grace begins at the Cross and ends at the Second Advent of Christ as He descends in Judgment to inaugurate His Kingdom reign. The Church Age begins at least fifty days after the Cross and concludes with the Rapture of the Church.

The following seven years of Tribulation are involved with God's judgments upon an unbelieving world and His preparation to bring Israel to Himself. It is nevertheless, still a period of Grace as is evident from a hundred and forty four thousand Jews being converted (Revelation 7:4), and *a great multitude, which no man could number, of all nations, and kindreds, and people, and tongues* (Revelation 7:9).

There can be no doubt that the Dispensation of the Kingdom begins officially with the descent of the victorious Lord Jesus

Christ as He comes with his saints and holy angels (2 Thessalonians 1:7 – 10; Revelation 19:11 – 16). He will defeat the Anti-Christ and his armies and bind Satan and cast him into the bottomless pit, where he will reside during the Millennial Kingdom. But even after Messiah has come, there will be a transitional period.

He will establish His throne in Jerusalem. If the Temple had to be cleansed when the Maccabees captured it from the Greeks, how much more will it need to be cleansed when taken from the Antichrist whose image was worshipped there? In fact, the Temple that will exist during the Tribulation will not be the same Temple that will grace the Millennium. Ezekiel takes great pains to describe that Temple in the final eight chapters of his book. Literalists agree that the Temple he describes is the Millennial Temple.

Could Messiah simply create a Temple with His word? Of course He could – but that has not been the pattern of God's dealing in the past. God employs men and allows them to be a part of what He is doing, and there is little doubt that that is the way He will build the Millennial Temple and set up His Kingdom as well.

How long will it take? Herod's Temple took forty years to complete. I am not arguing that the project will take that amount of time, but certainly there will be a significant period of time elapsed while the Millennial Temple is in construction.

Even the Government of the Kingdom seems to demand something of a transition. Messiah will rule, but He will rule through His saints and His people, Israel. We will rule and reign with Him, as will others who will be resurrected at the outset of the Kingdom (Revelation 20:4).

Responsibility will be determined by faithfulness in life (Luke 19:17), and appointment will be made accordingly. There is an extensive and complex system of government during this period and while the authority resides in Jerusalem, it extends over every portion of the earth. It will doubtless take time for that to be put in place.

Not only so, but the entire topography of the Middle East will be changed. Zechariah records how the Mount of Olives will divide to the north and to the south when touched by the Messiah's feet and form a great valley. A river will flow from the Throne down through that valley and bring life wherever it goes. It will be glorious indeed, but a major disruption of the existing topography, not to mention buildings, roads, and all else. It would be helpful to read again the entire fourteenth chapter of Zechariah.

Have you meditated on the significance of the judgments of the book of Revelation upon nature itself? Fountains and springs spewing forth poisonous and noxious water; a large portion of earth's vegetation destroyed; a significant part of sea creatures destroyed all of the debris of earthquakes and tsunamis to be cleaned up, and on and on I could go.

The Tribulation period will bring the greatest destruction of earth's ecological system and human civilization that has ever occurred short of Noah's flood. Could Messiah simply change all of that with a word – of course He could – but will He? He did not do so after the Flood and all former patterns suggest restoration and renovation will take its natural course.

Once the King sits upon David's throne, the Kingdoms of the earth must recognize Him and pay Him homage. Zechariah indicates that to demonstrate their submission they will be required to keep the Feast of Tabernacles in Jerusalem each year (Zechariah 14:16). There is also a penalty for those who might refuse or ignore the requirement. I think there is clear implication that bringing the entire earth under the full sovereignty of Messiah will be a process, and a process implies a time of transition.

Finally, and not insignificantly, will be the cleanup from two major wars. If we are correct that the battle of the northern confederacy with the Islamic nations will occur near the middle of the Tribulation week, then the seven years of cleanup predicted by

Ezekiel from that first battle will extend into the Millennial Kingdom.

On top of that will be the debris from the battle of Armageddon itself, a battle that engages the armies of the world with all of their armaments. How long will it take to clean that up?

All of these things considered, it is evident that the Kingdom will bring a notable transition period in hundreds of ways before the ideal is reached. Those who imagine that the earthly Millennial Kingdom will be perfected the moment Christ descends to the Mount of Olives, are ignoring the many indications of transitional development in that dispensation.

What, then, is the conclusion to all of this? While dispensations can be neatly divided by starting and terminal points, we need to recognize that from the human experience, dispensations tend to transition from one period to the next with many features overlapping. Often the saints take considerable time to fully grasp what God is doing, and the world around takes even longer.

The point of all of this is that we understand that vertical lines drawn on a chart may accurately mark the time of dispensational termination and change, but in experience, there will always be an indeterminate time of transition when the features of the new dispensational period are taking shape.

In out next two chapters we want to explore how this transitional principle works out in key New Testament books and how applying dispensational principles can help us over some of the problems we may encounter in textual interpretation.

CHAPTER TWENTY - TWO: DISPENSATIONAL PRINCIPLES IN MATTHEW

I once worked on a construction crew while attending college. One morning our foreman pulled a strange looking iron instrument out of the trunk of his car. "Here is a valuable tool," he told us. "But what is it?" we asked. "It is a new type of nail puller," he replied. "Does anyone know how to use it?" No one did, so we got a demonstration. It turned out to be a very useful tool once we saw how it worked. Your study of the dispensations will be priceless to you if you put it to work.

Pivotal Portions of Scripture
A survey of Bible passages that are most commonly misunderstood will disclose that these passages are in most cases found in the transitional periods from one dispensation to another.

There is still another troublesome type of passage that is found particularly in the Old Testament where both advents of Christ are in view and there seems to be no division between them. Because of that, there can be much confusion about the Second Advent of Christ.

Now it will not be possible to look at all of these difficulties, but I want to take several and show how applying dispensational principles to difficult passages can clear up the difficulty and make the Word clear and meaningful to us.

Looking at Matthew Dispensationally

For our purpose, we shall focus our attention upon the Gospel of Matthew. While Matthew is in what we call the New Testament, all of the events recorded, from the birth of Christ up to the Cross, happened during the old Dispensation of the Law.

This fact must be taken into account when interpreting these gospels, and if it is not there is a danger of concocting both wrong doctrine and wrong practice when we exegete these books. This becomes clearest in the gospel of Matthew and that is why I have directed our attention to it.

Before beginning, we need to keep these three facts in mind:

> (1) While Matthew is in the New Testament, all of the events recorded in Matthew from chapter 1 to chapter 27 happened during the old Dispensation of Law.

> (2) Christ was ministering solely to Israel during this period, not to Gentiles, and that fact is extremely important.

> (3) Finally, God is never taken by surprise. Christ knew ahead of time that the old Dispensation of the Law was about to end in His crucifixion and death, and therefore He reserved the last part of His ministry to prepare His disciples for the new Dispensation of Grace.

Now keeping these three facts in mind, let us move through Matthew's Gospel and touch the pivotal points in this book.

By carefully reading the Gospel of Matthew, you will observe that Christ is set forth as being Jewish in every respect. He is a descendent of Abraham, Isaac and Jacob (Mathew 1:1, 2). He stands in the lineage of David, thus making Him heir to David's throne. The first two chapters of this book deal primarily with the pedigree of the King of Israel.

Matthew prepares the way by presenting the credentials of Jesus the Messiah and King. He is the legal son of Joseph who, if the House of David was still reigning, would make Joseph the King rather than "the carpenter."

His Messianic identity is made clear by His birth in Bethlehem (Micah 5:2), and His royal lineage announced by the miraculous star that attends His birth and by both the Magi from the East coming to worship Him and Herod the King attempting to destroy Him as a rival (Matthew 2:1 – 18). It is evident in Matthew that the Holy Spirit, in superintending the writing of this book intended to demonstrate that Jesus, the Son of Mary, is the long promised Messiah, who is to deliver Israel and set up His glorious Kingdom (Isaiah 9:6, 7).

In chapters three and four we see the forerunner, John the Baptizer, preparing the way for the Kingdom. Notice carefully the message of John (3:2), and of Jesus (4:17), *the Kingdom of Heaven is at hand.* The signs of healing are His credentials proving that He was the King He claimed to be.

It is within this very Jewish setting that we find Christ ministering solely to Israel during the early chapters of Matthew's book When He speaks of the Kingdom, it is the one promised throughout the Tanach, or full text of the Hebrew Bible.

When He sets forth His standard of righteousness (Matthew 5 – 7) in the Sermon on the Mount, it is the righteousness of the promised Kingdom (Isaiah 11:4, 5). The requirement is heart righteousness, not merely perfunctory observance of external codes.

In chapters 8-10, the Kingdom is preached in Word and in mighty deeds. Miracles, which the rabbis had taught only Messiah would do, are performed, such as the healing of lepers, and raising of the dead. In addition, He shows to His disciples that He is Lord even of nature itself (Matthew 8:23 – 27).

In chapter 10 the band of followers is formed and sent out to preach the same message, namely, *the Kingdom of Heaven is at hand.* They are given power to perform these same Messianic miracles in order to demonstrate the truth of their proclamation. But they are specifically told:

> *Go not into the way of the Gentiles, and into any city of the Samaritans enter ye not: But go rather to the lost sheep of the house of Israel. And as ye go, preach, saying, The kingdom of heaven is at hand (*Matthew 10:5 – 7).

It is impossible to explain this apparent exclusiveness apart from understanding the nature of this transitional period. Jesus said, *Think not that I am come to destroy the law, or the prophets: I am not come to destroy, but to fulfill* (Matthew 5:17). So the prophets had promised a Kingdom to Israel and Messiah Jesus came and offered that Kingdom.

When we get to chapters eleven to thirteen, we reach the transitional chapters of this gospel. In Chapter 11 we see several things taking place. First, while Jesus' disciples were preaching the message of the Kingdom throughout the Jewish countryside, John the Baptist, the forerunner of the King (and last in the line of the prophets of the old dispensation), was arrested and thrown into prison by Herod (Matthew 11:2–15). This signals overt opposition toward the King (Jesus), the Kingdom, and John, the King's herald. A turn in the road has occurred.

Jesus acknowledges John and even said that his ministry could have fulfilled the prophecy of Elijah's coming if Israel would have received it. However, Israel did not receive the message and prepare by repentance for the imminent Kingdom, as becomes evident in the laments of verses 20 – 24, where Jesus upbraids the people for refusing the Kingdom by lack of repentance:

> *Then began he to upbraid the cities wherein most of his mighty works were done, because they repented not: Woe unto thee, Chorazin! woe unto thee, Bethsaida! for if the mighty works, which were done in you, had been done in Tyre and Sidon, they would have repented long ago in sackcloth and ashes. But I say unto you, It shall be more tolerable for Tyre and Sidon at the day of judgment, than for you. And thou, Capernaum, which art exalted unto heaven, shalt be brought down to hell: for if the mighty works, which have been done in thee, had been done in Sodom, it would have remained until this day. But I say unto you, That it shall be more tolerable for the land of Sodom in the day of judgment, than for thee* (Matthew 11:20 – 24).

Notice again that these are Jews rejecting a Kingdom, not a mixture of people rejecting the gospel of salvation. But now, after this rejection, and for the first time, Jesus offers a message of personal commitment and salvation (11:28-30). Israel as a whole has rejected the Kingdom and now the invitation is given to individuals to personally receive the King.

In chapter twelve, he declares His person – who He is. Though rejected, He is, greater than the Temple (and all it stood for i.e.; Matthew 12:6); greater than the prophets (verse 41) Jonah being representative, and greater than Israel's greatest king, i.e., Solomon (verse 42).

Furthermore, chapter twelve deals with the irreconcilable controversy with the religious leaders who not only reject the King but claim that His power is of the Devil (12:24). If the credentials He offers (i.e., the Messianic miracles), are ascribed to Satan, the possibility of faith in the Person performing those miracles is removed and Israel's leaders have reached a logical impasse.

The result is that Jesus announces that human relationships are going to be put aside in favor of spiritual relationships (12:46-50). It will no longer be important to be merely a son of Abraham (a Jew) after the flesh, but Christ will now respect only those who are "sons of Abraham" by faith in Him.

So in chapter thirteen a significant transition occurs. He goes *out of the house* and sits down in a boat upon the sea, and begins to tell His followers how the Kingdom will manifest itself in "Mystery" form during this present age. Since the King and the Kingdom have been rejected by Israel, Jesus explains what form the Kingdom will take during the coming Dispensation of Grace. It will not come with *outward show* but only in the hearts of those who own His sovereignty over their lives.

In chapters fourteen and fifteen, the record begins with the execution of John the Baptist and portends similar treatment for the Messiah Himself. But, beginning in these chapters we see Jesus' attention now directed to the training of His disciples for the work ahead.

In chapter sixteen, Jesus begins to talk of His Church rather than His Kingdom (16:18), and it will be built upon His person (16:16) and His work of redemption (16:21). It is obvious that the disciples do not understand this transition from a Kingdom to a Church, and this becomes plainer with every succeeding chapter.

However, and this is a point we must not miss, the promised Kingdom may be postponed, but it is not forgotten. In chapter 17 Jesus takes His three intimates up to a mountain and is transfigured before them in all the glory of the Kingdom. The "take away" from this event is recorded by Peter in his second epistle:

> *For we have not followed cunningly devised fables, when we made known unto you the power and coming of our Lord Jesus Christ, but were eyewitnesses of his majesty. For he received from God the Father honour and glory, when there came such a voice to him from the excellent glory, This is*

my beloved Son, in whom I am well pleased. And this voice which came from heaven we heard, when we were with him in the holy mount (2 Peter 1:16 – 18).

Peter understood the event as a preview of things to come. The Kingdom that was prophesied is coming and so is the King. Not only does Scripture promise it, but Peter got a preview of it on the mount. But after this event Christ speaks more and more of the Church and His death and less and less of the Kingdom.

Chapter twenty one reveals Jesus' official presentation of Himself as King to Israel (see Zechariah 9:9), but the verdict is already in, and this action only makes His rejection by the rulers official (21:15). This in turn leads to three chapters of controversy with the Jewish leaders and parables concerning the Kingdom which will come in the future.

Chapters twenty four and twenty five, continue Jesus' prophecy of how the Kingdom will come, but notice that this whole passage deals with the coming Kingdom, not the Church, and is fulfilled in the Tribulation and the Millennium. This leads to His death in chapter twenty seven, which ends the old dispensation. The new dispensation opens in chapter twenty eight, with a victorious resurrection shout and a command to take the gospel of forgiveness and salvation to the whole world.

By looking at Matthew dispensationally, we have seen how God was leading those who believed and trusted Christ through this transitional period, preparing them at every turn for the next step. At the same time, he honestly offering the prophesied Kingdom to a sinful nation that God knew would reject it and crucify the King.

Like a rose unfolding its petals to reveal the secret beauty within, the Gospel of Matthew has a peculiar beauty as it unfolds the dispensational plan of God. It is no longer just a collection of random reminiscences concerning the life of Christ. It is the doorway into a new dispensation and into the New Testament itself.

CHAPTER TWENTY - THREE:
DISPENSATIONAL PRINCIPLES IN ACTS

Another pivotal portion of Scripture is the book of Acts. The entire book is transitional in nature, taking us from the question of the disciples in chapter one: *Wilt Thou at this time restore again the Kingdom to Israel* (Acts 1:6)?, to the final declaration of Paul: *Be it known therefore unto you* (Jews), *that the salvation of God is sent unto the Gentiles, and that they will hear it* (Acts 28:28).

Thus, Acts transitions us through Israel's rejection of the Gospel message, to the full establishment of the Church, now made up primarily of Gentile believers. We pass from the early chapters of Jewish domination, in which the Church held to both cultural and Mosaic features, to a Gentile leadership, free to exercise it new liberty in Christ, as the book reaches its conclusion.

Failure to recognize this is fatal in any attempt to interpret the message of the book. Failure to recognize this is the reason attempts are made today to establish some event in the book of Acts as a norm for church life now.

There are also a variety of ways and situations in Acts in which the Holy Spirit is received or given and these can become perplexing and confusing as well. It is several of these I want to examine and as we do, we will employ those principles which can help us understand the whole book. .

In Acts chapter two, Peter offers the gift of the Holy Spirit to those who will repent and submit to baptism. In Acts eight, the Holy Spirit was given only after the laying on of hands of the Jewish Apostles, and in Acts ten the Holy Spirit is received immediately upon hearing and believing the gospel message. Why the difference? Which, if any is the norm?

Only by approaching these passages from a dispensational point of view can we construct a plausible answer. All those to the contrary notwithstanding, these instances are not the pattern for either salvation or receiving the Spirit during this age.

In attempting to interpret any passage several questions are essential: (1) Precisely what does the text say? (2) Exactly who is being addressed in this passage? (3) Has any situation preceded what is recorded here that may have a bearing upon this text? Let's consider those questions as we examine this and several additional passages in Acts.

To begin with, we must keep in mind that as the book of Acts opens. God has been dealing with the nation of Israel exclusively since Genesis chapter twelve. If there is going to be a major transition from *the Jew first* to *also the Greek* (Gentile), we should expect to see it take place in this book.

The Demand of Acts 2
Let's think about what happened in Acts chapter two. Only Jews were present at Pentecost (see Acts 2:5). That means that Peter's message that day was addressed to no one but Jews. And think about it – these were some of the same Jews that had, not two months previously, cried, *Away with him, crucify Him, we have no king but Caesar*. The Jewish nation had officially and publicly, rejected the claims of Christ and crucified Him as an imposter (see John 19:15; Matthew 27:63).

Now reading Peter's message (Acts 2:14-36), in the light of this fact, places what he said in a whole new light. Peter explicitly and unequivocally lays the responsibility for Jesus' death on the Jewish nation and on their leaders.
Consider what he says:

> *Ye men of Israel, hear these words; Jesus of Nazareth, a man approved of God among you by miracles and wonders and signs, which God did by him in the midst of you, as ye yourselves also know: Him, being delivered by the determinate counsel and foreknowledge of God, <u>ye have taken, and by wicked hands have crucified and slain</u>: Whom God hath raised up, having loosed the pains of death: because it was not possible that he should be holden of it* (Acts 2:22 – 24).

Or this:

> *Therefore let all the house of Israel know assuredly, that God hath made that same Jesus, <u>whom ye have crucified, both Lord and Christ</u>* (Acts 2:36).

Please note the key phrases; *Ye men of Israel,* and *let all the house of Israel know, etc.* This message is to Jews only and even more precisely, it is to the nation – the same nation that had officially and explicitly denied Him and called for His death. Those who were listening were a part of that nation and therefore, implicitly a part of that action. The response was electrifying.

> *Now when they heard this, they were pricked in their heart, and said unto Peter and to the rest of the apostles, Men and brethren, what shall we do* (Acts 2:37)?

That is, "Seeing our national leaders have done this awful deed, how *can* we escape the certain judgment that must be upon us from God?"

Peter's answer then is appropriate to the people as well as to the question. He says;

> *Repent, and be baptized every one of you in the name of Jesus Christ for the remission of sins, and ye shall receive the gift of the Holy Ghost. For the promise is unto you, and to your children, and to all that are afar off, even as many as the Lord our God shall call. And with many other words did he testify and exhort, saying,* <u>Save yourselves from this untoward generation</u> (Acts 2:38 – 40).

Notice, Peter's message was not only "be saved from your sins," although it certainly included this, but it was also *save yourselves from this untoward generation;* that is, from this nation that publicly and officially rejected Messiah Jesus. And the result would be that they would receive the *gift of the Holy Ghost*, the manifestation to the Jews that they were accepted by God.

Please remember, that this nation of people had, not two months before this, publicly and officially declared Christ an imposter and a fraud, and crucified Him. The need was not only repentance from sins generally, but repentance from the crime of crucifying the Son of God, and that repentance would require public and personal repudiation of what their leaders had done, by being baptized in the name of the very One they had denied.

God could hardly place His approval on members of that nation until they publicly and personally repudiated their national leaders and their previous decision. This was likely what necessitated them to be baptized, making this public confession of Christ and repudiation of the actions of their rulers, before they could be acknowledged by God by being given the gift of the Holy Spirit.

Notice however, this was a unique experience. It never happened again. In no other place, in the book of Acts or elsewhere, was anyone required to be baptized before receiving salvation or the gift of the Holy Spirit. Yet there are denominations that teach baptism is essential for salvation based on this passage.

To make this, as some do, a pattern case for this dispensation and make it apply to everyone is to fail to *rightly divide the Word of Truth*. The dispensationalist by understanding the nature of these transitional passages and by a close adherence to the words of the text can avoid that kind of error.

The Delay of Acts 8
Now let's take a look at Acts chapter eight. The background for the passage is the scattering of the disciples that took place as a result of the martyrdom of Stephen and the persecution led by Saul of Tarsus. Driven from Jerusalem and its environs, the disciples scattered to find safety, but preached the Word wherever they went.

One of the company was a deacon named Philip – often referred to as Philip the evangelist. A short while later, he would be used of God to open the African continent to Christ as a result of bringing to faith the treasurer of Candace, queen of the Ethiopians. But his first stop was in Samaria.

What makes this a crucial passage is the delay experienced by the Samaritans in receiving the Holy Spirit after they had believed and were baptized. The passage in question is as follows:

> *Now when the apostles which were at Jerusalem heard that Samaria had received the word of God, they sent unto them Peter and John: Who, when they were come down, prayed for them, that they might receive the Holy Ghost: (For as yet he was fallen upon none of them: only they were baptized in the name of the Lord Jesus.) Then laid they their hands on them, and they received the Holy Ghost* (Acts 8:14 – 17).

Once again there are those who attempt to use this passage as a proof text to teach that the Holy Spirit can only be imparted by the laying on of hands. Some teach that the hands must be those of an Apostle and so teach what is called Apostolic succession, which claims that there is a viable Apostolate today.

While this leads us into another subject that cannot be addressed here, suffice it to say that there is neither biblical nor historic proof of Apostolic Succession, nor is there present proof that a valid Apostolate exists in our time. The defining litmus test for any church is not the presence of a living Apostle, but its conformity to the Word of God.

So why then did it require the laying on of the Apostles hands in this particular case? Our recourse to answer that question is, as always, the text, both the immediate text and corresponding ones. Only if we ask our questions can we hope to reach a correct understanding.

To begin with where did this take place? It took place in Samaria. What possible significance is there to that? The place is first mentioned by name in 1 Kings 13:32. It was founded by Omri who was King of Israel and head of a dynasty that brought forth the likes of Ahab and Jezebel; some of the most wicked of Israel's royalty.

As the capitol of the northern kingdom, it became a center of idolatry and the location of the temple of Baal. However, it also saw God's miraculous deliverances under the ministry of both Elijah and Elisha, which included the healing of Naaman, the Syrian captain, of his leprosy.

In 722 BC, Samaria was conquered after a long (three year) siege by Shalmaneser, the king of Assyria. He deported much of the population and repopulated the area as recorded in 2 Kings chapter seventeen.

> *And the king of Assyria brought men from Babylon, and from Cuthah, and from Ava, and from Hamath, and from Sepharvaim, and placed them in the cities*

of Samaria instead of the children of Israel: and they possessed Samaria, and dwelt in the cities thereof (2 Kings 17:24).

This same passage goes on to tell of the Assyrian King's attempt to protect the people he had resettled from the attacks of wild beasts by teaching them *the manner of the God of the land* (vs. 26). To accomplish this, the king sent one of the former Samaritan priests to instruct them.

Samaritan priests were already compromised by idolatry which had led to the captivity in the first place, and the result was the subsequent total confusion of the religious practice of the entire area. It was the descendants of this group of people, who had by then thoroughly mixed with those of Jewish heritage, that Nehemiah encountered when he came to rebuild the city of Jerusalem.

Being shut out from that enterprise and from the rebuilt Jewish Temple, they later built a temple of their own and established the synchronistic form of Hebrewistic religion which existed in Christ's time. It was that which Jesus Christ encountered when he sat on Jacob's well in Sychar and talked with the woman of Samaria. It is here we get a hint as to why the initial visitation of the gospel to that region occurred as it did.

When Jesus confronted the sin of the woman at the well, she replied, *Sir, I perceive that thou art a prophet. Our fathers worshipped in this mountain; and ye say, that in Jerusalem is the place where men ought to worship* (John 4:19, 20). What her words revealed was that Samaritans had established a whole system of religion that was in opposition to that at Jerusalem.

An interesting question here might be to ask; Was she correct? – that is, had *her fathers* (and all Jewish fathers) worshipped in that mount? Indeed they had. Joshua built the first altar after entering the land on Mt. Ebal immediately after the conquest of Ai (Joshua 8:30 – 35).

So the Samaritans had taken that historic fact and used it to attempt to bolster their claim for their own temple and religious practice. Jesus set the matter straight with these words, *Ye worship ye know not what: we know what we worship: for salvation is of the Jews* (John 4:22).

In this passage, it appears that God wanted that issue resolved so that it would never come up in the Church in the future. So, before these Samaritans could receive the Holy Spirit, they had to submit to the laying on of the hands of Jewish Apostles – *salvation is of the Jews.*

The Disciples in Acts 19
The situation of the laying on of hands to receive the Holy Spirit occurs in only one other place and for a totally different reason. In Acts chapter nineteen, the Apostle Paul came to Ephesus. There as his manner had been in every place, he entered the synagogue and found twelve men, all evidently Jews, who had been deeply influenced by the ministry of Apollos (to whom we are introduced in the closing verses of the previous chapter).

What we know of Apollos and his ministry is that he was, *a certain Jew . . . born at Alexandria.* His birthplace explains his Grecian name for Alexandria was a thoroughly Hellenized city.

We further read of him that he was, *an eloquent man, and mighty in the scriptures.* We are also told that he came to Ephesus and that he *was instructed in the way of the Lord; and being fervent in the spirit, he spake and taught diligently the things of the Lord, <u>knowing only the baptism of John</u>* (Acts 18:24, 25).

Apollos had received the baptism of repentance administered by John the Baptist. This was a baptism for Jewish believers who wished to repent and prepare themselves for the Messianic Kingdom which John was announcing. Apollos had received this baptism, and believed fervently in what John had preached, and so he preached the same message in Ephesus and these twelve men responded by receiving the baptism of repentance in anticipation of the Kingdom.

When Paul learned of their situation, he told them, "the rest of the story." He told them of Messiah's rejection, His crucifixion, His resurrection and the subsequent coming of the Holy Spirit to form a new thing – the Church, the Body of Christ.

When they believed Paul's message they were re-baptized. Why? Because John's baptism was related to Israel and the promise of a coming Messianic Kingdom, while Christian baptism is an identification with Christ in His finished work of redemption – two entirely different ideas.

Once again we are called upon to distinguish things that differ. Dispensationalists are often criticized for that very practice, but Scripture on the other hand, tells us that *he that is spiritual judgeth* (Strong: **anakrinō** scrutinize, investigate, interrogate, determine: - ask, question, discern, examine, judge, search) *all things* (1 Corinthians 2:15). There is simply a difference in these two baptisms even though ministered in the same manner. Therefore, Paul re-baptized these twelve men.

Now the issue that had brought all this about was the apparent lack of evidence in the lives of these men that they had received the Holy Spirit. Although John had preached that the One coming after him would *baptize you with the Holy Spirit and with fire* (Matthew 3:11), it seems this had not been a part of Apollos' preaching.

It was for this very purpose then that Paul brought them along to faith in the redemptive work of Messiah. It for this purpose that Paul completed their commitment by baptizing them in Christian baptism, *and when Paul had laid hands on them the Holy Ghost came on them, and they spake with tongues and prophesied* (Acts 19:6).

The phrase, *the Holy Ghost came on them,* is significant. It does not indicate the same thing as we saw in Acts 8:17 where *they received* (Gr. **lambano**) *the Holy Spirit*. It rather suggests the enabling of the Spirit for service. It was a phrase common to those in former dispensations where the

Spirit came upon them to enable them for a certain task of ministry (see Judges 14:6).

What seems to have occurred here is that upon believing the message, the Holy Spirit performed all His sovereign works of regeneration, indwelling, sealing and baptizing these men into the Body of Christ. In addition, as Paul lays his hands on them, they are given Spiritual enablements for ministry.

The important point to be observed, however, is that this action of the Apostle Paul is not the norm for this age. Acts is a transitional book that is carrying us from the beginning phases of one dispensation to its full development.

The Apostolic office died with the last of the first century Apostles. The Holy Spirit is received in this age the moment a sinner places his faith fully in Christ. Spiritual enablement follows as we yield to the Spirit, obey the Spirit and are thus filled with the Spirit (Ephesians 5:18).

Allow me then to exhort you as Paul did; *he that is spiritual judgeth* (Strong: **anakrinō** scrutinize, investigate, interrogate, determine: - ask, question, discern, examine, judge, search) *all things* (1 Corinthians 2:15). Distinguish the ages – discern things that differ. And whatever you do, be a servant to the text. Listen to what it is saying. Do not drag its unwilling utterances to fit your preconceived ideas. Let the text of Scripture conform you to itself.

Put these dispensational principles to work and you will find a *new* pleasure and thrill in the study of God's Word. In our final chapter we shall see how a study of the dispensations can give a larger understanding of God, of man, of grace, and of the Bible itself.

CHAPTER TWENTY - FOUR:
DISPENSATIONALISM
- What We Can Learn

We saw in the last two chapters that our dispensational study can provide a useful tool to an understanding of the Word of God. However, we must always remember that tools are not enough.

Missionary and author Godfrey Bull wrote a story of his personal experiences and thoughts during his imprisonment by the Communists in China from October, 1950, to December, 1953. The book was titled; *God Holds the Key*.

In it he compares the Bible to a wonderful country. This country is ruled by the "Authority" or God Himself. Entrance to the country is very often misunderstood.

Mr. Bull writes, "Many dignitaries of scholarship, experts of scientific standing and critics of acclaimed ability arrive daily at the frontier stations and present their special credentials." These, he tells us, are almost all refused. "What is required is a bona fide declaration of the intention of the entrant. This includes an indication of an attitude of faith in, and submission to, the Authority, and a willingness to act on the information obtained." [1]

What Godfrey Bull is saying may be summed up in two verses of Scripture, *But the natural man receiveth not the things of the Spirit of God: for they are foolishness unto him: neither can he know them, because they are spiritually discerned* (1 Corinthians 2:14). Therefore, to understand the Word we must be saved. Impressive credentials will never substitute for a heart of faith.

The second is found in James 1:22, *But obey the message; be doers of the Word, and not merely listeners to it, betraying yourselves into deception by reasoning contrary to the truth"* (Amplified New Testament). 2

We must be prepared to submit. With these attitudes of faith and obedience we can use the tools and find *wondrous things out of Thy Law* (Psalm 119:18).

What Dispensational Study Teaches Us About God

Postmodernism leaves its adherents in a state of ambivalent uncertainty. If there is a God, he has allowed things to somehow get out of control. Many seem to be waiting for something, they hardly know what, that will clean up the mess.

Christians, we find, are not immune to similar attitudes. While believing that God has things under control, many seem to think He is simply sitting back and waiting for man to do enough good to bring in the Kingdom.

A study of the dispensational divisions of Scripture demonstrates that God is not sitting around waiting for anything, certainly not for our assistance. He is actively at work, carrying out a Divine purpose in this age as He has in every other. This study proves that God is both omniscient and omnipotent, and One Who is never taken by surprise, but has preceded man in every age, planning and working and proving His love.

He has also disclosed, through every conceivable test, man's weakness and sinfulness and inability to govern even himself. God is a God of order, for He is never "ruffled." He is a God of patience, for He is never hurried. He is a God of power, for He is never frustrated. He is a God of wisdom, for He is never wrong. He is a God of righteousness, for He is never unfair. He is a God of grace, for He is never unloving.

It was an examination of God's dispensational dealings with Israel, in spite of all that nation's failures, that caused Paul to say in Romans 11:33, *0 the depth of the riches both of the wisdom and knowledge of God! How unsearchable are his judgments, and his ways past finding out!* And it is a realization of God's dispensational plan for the Gentiles that caused James to exalt, *Known unto God are all his works from the beginning of the world* (Acts 15:18). Our God has become to us a bigger God, a greater God, and a God worthy of all our trust and praise.

If God has a plan for the ages and He is able to execute that plan, is it not reasonable to believe that God can carry out His plan for our lives? It is this that allows us to say, *My times are in Thy hands* (Psalm 31:15), and say it with peace and confidence. It is this perfect plan, and this unerring wisdom, that reminds us that *it is God which worketh in you both to will and to do of his good pleasure* (Philippians 2:13).

If we are not convinced of that truth after a study like this, we are not likely to ever be convinced. It is all the evidence I need when I see Abraham, standing alone under a starry sky, thousands of years ago, and listening to God make promises to him of his future down to the end of time. Then I look around and see God's promises to that one man being fulfilled before my eyes. No wonder I can say, *we have a strong consolation, who have fled for refuge to lay hold upon the hope set before us* (Hebrews 6:18).

What Dispensational Study Teaches Us About Man

After watching man's performance through the seven great dispensational periods, it is impossible for us to ever again believe in that humanistic theory that man has a divine "spark" which only needs to be fanned and it will blaze into the flame of divinity. If we learned a single thing in these studies, it is that man is corrupt. He is incurably corrupt. He is totally depraved and sinful and under no condition can he do right or please God.

Our study will set us free from the dream of certain liberal preachers and philosophers that man needs only the right environment to be the right kind of man. We are certain, before they try, that new houses, new clothes, new gardens, new occupations or new identities will not make new men. *Man* is so depraved that only the new birth (John 3) can transform him. He must be a new creation. Perhaps we already knew this truth, but our study of the dispensations should have engraved it upon our hearts (as well as our minds), so deeply that we will never forget it.

What Dispensational Study Teaches Us About Law And Grace

A study of the dispensations helps us see clearly that the principles of law and grace are forever separate and cannot be mingled (Romans 4:1-8; 11:6). As dispensationalists, we understand that Law is God demanding from man what he cannot produce while Grace is God giving man what he does not deserve; that is, salvation and eternal life and fellowship with Himself both now and for eternity.

From the knowledge we have gained of man, we recognize that any scheme of self-effort for man is doomed to failure from the beginning. This is a valuable conviction because it can save us from the legalistic teachers of this age that make either salvation or sanctification contingent upon the Old Testament Law or the Sermon on the Mount or some ordinance, such as baptism. *And if* [it be] *by grace, then is it no more of works: otherwise grace is no more grace. But if it be of works, then is it no more grace: otherwise work is no more work* (Romans 11:6).

What Dispensational Study Teaches Us About The Present and The Future

In Dispensational study, we learn to distinguish the ages. We recognize that from Genesis chapter twelve to Acts chapter ten, the Jew is largely in view. We learn that God has a special program with Israel, different from His program for the Church.

We do not have to explain away the promises of god that have not yet been fulfilled. We can have absolute confidence that every promise will be fulfilled and in the exact terms in which it was given.

The Bible is no longer a heterogeneous collection of writings, but a harmony, a whole, a grand and glorious story of the ages of God's dealing with man.

We also understand God's plan for this age. He is not "building a kingdom," as some would have us believe. He is *taking out from among the Gentiles a people for his name* (Acts 15:14).

We see that God is utterly consistent, that He is not whimsical in His dealing but orderly, and that He is carrying out His plan for each age in a measured and harmonious way.

Furthermore, we are saved from confusing the plan and responsibilities of one dispensation with the plan and responsibilities of another. In short, we are *rightly dividing the Word of Truth* (2 Timothy 2:15).

What Dispensational Study Teaches Us About The Bible

In no other approach to the Scriptures do we see with quite the same clarity the inspiration and accuracy of the Bible. Dispensational study demands that we adhere to the text and receive it in its historical and grammatical sense. The theme of a true dispensationalist is "the text, the text, the text."

As we study the dispensations we can grasp the Divine pattern of Scripture, like the theme of a great symphony, running from the beginning to the end and relating each part to the whole plan of God. All Scripture is for us, but not all is written to us. We learn to distinguish things that differ – we learn to *rightly divide the Word of Truth*.

Finally, although dispensational study can indeed open the Scriptures to us, we must always be careful not to allow our knowledge to destroy the humility of the Spirit. *Knowledge puffeth up, but love edifieth* (1 Corinthians 8:1). If our study has allowed us to see clearer in order that we might love or serve Him better, it will be of tremendous value.

APPENDIX

We reproduce here "the messages to the seven churches" found on page 1331 of the Scofield Reference Bible (1909 ed,).

The messages to the seven churches have a fourfold application: (1) <u>Local</u>, to the churches actually addressed; (2) <u>admonitory</u>, to all churches in all time as tests by which they may discern their true spiritual state in the sight of God; (3) <u>personal</u>, in the exhortations to him "that hath an ear," and in the promises "to him that overcometh"; (4) <u>prophetic</u>, as disclosing seven phases of the *spiritual* history of the church from, say, A.D. 96 to the end. It is incredible that in a prophecy covering the church period there should be no such foreview. These messages must contain that foreview if it is in the book at all, for the church does not appear after 3:22. Again, these messages by their very terms go beyond the local assemblies mentioned. Most conclusively of all, these messages do present an exact foreview of the *spiritual* history of the church, and in this precise order. Ephesus gives the general state at the date of the writing; Smyrna, the period of the great persecutions; Pergamos, the church settled down in the world, "where Satan's throne is," after the conversion of Constantine, say, A.D. 316. Thyatira is the Papacy, developed out of the Pergamos state: Balaamism (worldliness) and Nicolaitanism (priestly assumption) having conquered. As Jezebel brought idolatry into Israel, so Romanism weds Christian doctrine to pagan ceremonies. Sardis is the Protestant Reformation, whose works were not "fulfilled." Philadelphia is whatever bears clear testimony to the Word and the Name in the time of self-satisfied profession represented by Laodicea.

FOOTNOTES

Chapter 1: INTRODUCTION

1. (Tragedy of Macbeth; Scene V).

2. Article on Post-Modernism, D.P. Teague http://www.postmodernpreaching.net/

3. Ibid cited

4. Ibid

5. David L. Larsen, *Is God a Dispensationalist?* (Kearney, NE; Morris Publishing (2008) p.17

6. John Godfrey Saxe *Six Blind Men & The Elephant* (1816-1887) http://en.wikipedia.org/wiki/Blind_men_and_an_Elephant

Chapter 2: DEFINING TERMS

1. Dr. John MacArthur, *Bible Study 101* Lesson 8, www.suite101.com

2. Thomas Ice; *The Thomas Ice Collection: A Brief History of Premillennialism* https://www.raptureready.com/featured/ice/AShortHistoryOfDispensationalism.html

3. Larry V. Crutchfield, *Ages and Dispensations of the Ante-Nicene Fathers* http://www.galaxie.com/article/bsac144-576-02

4. 1687, Pierre Poiret *The Divine Economy: Or, a Universal System of the Works and Purposes of God Towards Men, Demonstrated;* six volumes (1687)

5. Charles Caldwell Ryrie, *Dispensationalism Today* (Chicago)Moody Press, (1965) cited p. 76

6. Donald Grey Barnhouse *Teaching the Word of Truth*; William B. Eerdmans Publishing Company, 1958; pp. 185, 186

Chapter 3: GETTING STARTED

1. Dr. A.T. Pierson *Keys to the Word: or, Helps to Bible Study* (1887) Pamphlet

Chapter 4: THE DISPENSATION OF INNOCENCE

1. Renald E. Showers, *There Really Is A Difference*; Friends of Israel Gospel Ministry, Inc. (1990) p. 33

Chapter 5: THE DISPENSATION OF CONSCIENCE

1. Noah Webster published dictionary (1828), copyright on April 14.

Chapter 6: THE DISPENSATION OF HUMAN GOVERNMENT

1. Robert Knight (article) http://onenewsnow.com/perspectives/robert-knight/2015/01/27

2. Robert S. Candlish *Book of Genesis*; (Edinburg) Adam & Charles Black (1868) vol. 1

3. Alexander Hislop *The Two Babylons* (New York NY) Loizeaux Brothers, Inc. (1953)

4. Jay Jackendoff; *How Did Human Language Begin?* http://www.linguisticsociety.org/files/LanguageBegin.pdf

Chapter 7: THE DISPENSATION OF PROMISE

1. C. I. Scofield, *The Scofield Reference Bible* (New York) Oxford University Press (1909) p. 19

2. Adam Clark; *Adam Clark's Commentary on the Bible*, (E-Sword)

Chapter 10: THE PURPOSE OF THE LAW

1. John Bunyan, *The Pilgrim's Progress*, (New York) Rinehart & Co., Inc. (1948) p. 24

2. C. I. Scofield, *The Scofield Reference Bible* (New York) Oxford University Press (1909) p. 1194

Chapter 11: THE DISPENSATION OF GRACE – Some Vital Explanations

1. Renald E. Showers, *There Really Is A Difference*; Friends of Israel Gospel Ministry, Inc. (1990) p. 170

2. Dr. John MacArthur, *Bible Study 101* Lesson 8, www.suite101.com

3. C. I. Scofield, *The Scofield Reference Bible* (New York) Oxford University Press (1909) p. 1014

4. Ibid. p. 1252

4. C. I. Scofield, Rightly Dividing The Word of Truth, (1896), Updated, Advanced Biblical Studies, Source of Light Ministries, Int. (2014) p. 47

Chapter 12: THE DISPENSATION OF GRACE – Analyzed

1. Author unknown

2. Author uncertain; Attributed to C. H. Spurgeon; http://www.preceptaustin.org/accepted_in_the_beloved.htm

3. C. I. Scofield, *Rightly Dividing The Word of Truth*, (1896), Updated, Advanced Biblical Studies, Source of Light Ministries, Int. (2014) p. 70

4. Outline by Dr. Ralph H. Stoll (Pamphlet)

Chapter 13: THE DISPENSATION OF GRACE – The Failure – Apostasy

1. Harry Emerson Fosdick, *Shall the Fundamentalists Win?* Sermon, (May 1922 letter dated January 31, 1948).

2. Nels F. S. Ferre, *The Christian Understanding of God*, Harper & Brothers Publishers, New York, NY (1951) p. 191

3. Bishop James A. Pike, Pastoral letter to Episcopal Churches of California, (circa 1964).

4. Marcus Borg, *The God We Never Knew,* (New York, NY: Harper Collins, First Harper Collins Paperback Edition, 1998), p. 25

5. Brian McLaren, *Church on the Other Side,* (Grand Rapids, MI: Zondervan, 2003) p. 239

6. Alan Jones, *Reimagining Christianity* (Hoboken, NJ: Wiley and Sons, 2005), p. 168

7. William Shannon, *Silence on Fire* (New York, NY: The Crossroad Publishing Company 1995 edition), pp. 109-110

8. J. Dwight Pentecost; *Things to Come*; Dunham Publishing Company, Finley Ohio; (1958); p. 237

Chapter 15: THE DISPENSATION OF THE KINGDOM – Analyzing the Final Dispensation

1. John C. Whitcomb *Christ's Atonement and Animal Sacrifices in Israel,* Grace Theological Journal 6.2, (1985), pp 201 – 217

2. David L. Larsen, *Is God a Dispensationalist?* Kearney, NE; Morris Publishing (2008) pp. 122, 123

3. J. Dwight Pentecost; *Things to Come*; Dunham Publishing Company, Finley Ohio; (1958); pp.503

4. George N. H. Peters, *The Theocratic Kingdom*, Grand Rapids, Michigan: Kregel Publications, (1952); 3 vols.

5. J. Dwight Pentecost; *Things to Come*; Dunham Publishing Company, Finley Ohio; (1958); pp 482

Chapter 16: MAKING DISPENSATIONAL DISTINCTIONS

1. C. I. Scofield, Rightly Dividing The Word of Truth, (1896), Updated, Advanced Biblical Studies, Source of Light Ministries, Int. (2014)

2. David L. Larsen, *Is God a Dispensationalist?* (Kearney, NE; Morris Publishing (2008) p. 20

Chapter 17: SALVATION IN DISPENSATIONALISM

1. Biblical Ministries Worldwide *On This We Stand* (Brochure)

Chapter 18: DISPENSATIONAL PERSPICUITY

1. Hank Hanegraaff *The Perspicuity of Scripture* Christian Research Institute Perspective; www.equip.org/**perspectives**/the-**perspicuity**-of-**scri**pture
2. George E. Ladd, Critical Questions About the Kingdom of God (Grand Rapids: Wm. B. Eerdmans Publishing Co., (1952), p. 49

Chapter 19: DISPENSATIONAL VS. COVENANT THEOLOGY

1. R. S. Clark, *History of Covenant Theology* (2001) www.spindleworks.com/library/CR/clark.htm

2. Gary Gilley, *New Calvinism*; Think on These Things (Article) Southern View Chapel, Springfield, Ill. January/February - 2015, Volume 21, Issue 1

3. C. I. Scofield, *The Scofield Reference Bible* (New York) Oxford University Press (1909) reference chain begins on p. 5

4. Gary Gilley, New Calvinism; Think on These Things (Article) Southern View Chapel, Springfield, Ill. January/February - 2015, Volume 21, Issue 1

5. Covenant_theology https://en.wikipedia.org/wiki/

Chapter 20: THE CHURCH AGE – A PARENTHESIS IN PROPHECY

1. Bill Shade, *The Prophetic Destiny of Israel & the Islamic Nations*, Madison, GA Globe Publishers (2014) p. 106

2. Ibid. pp. 106, 107

3. Sir Robert Anderson, *The Coming Prince;* Kregel Publishing Company, Grand Rapids, Michigan; (1954) p. 124

4. John Gill's Exposition of the Entire Bible

5. (Albert Barnes Notes on the Bible : online)

6. Clarence B. Bass, *Backgrounds to Dispensationalism* (Grand Rapids: Eerdmans, 1960) 26ff

7. David L. Larsen, *Is God a Dispensationalist?* (Kearney, NE; Morris Publishing (2008) p. 59

Chapter 24: DISPENSATIONALISM: WHAT WE CAN LEARN

1. Godfrey T. Bull, *God Holds the Key*; London: Hodder & Stoughton (1959) p. ref. uncertain

Appendix

1. C. I. Scofield, *The Scofield Reference Bible* (New York) Oxford University Press (1909) p. 1331

ABOUT THE AUTHOR:

Born in Altoona, Pennsylvania, Dr. Shade completed studies at Philadelphia Bible Institute and Wheaton College. He began serving in faith missionary work in 1956 with *Scripture Memory Mountain Mission* in Southeastern Kentucky, where he regularly ministered to 10,000 teenagers in seven counties through the high school ministry. During the same time, he became pastor of McRoberts Missionary Baptist Church where he served for eight years.

In 1964, Dr. Shade moved to York, Pennsylvania, where he founded and directed the *Grace and Truth Evangelistic Association* which was active in radio and television ministry, evangelistic campaigns, and camp/conference ministries. He was the founder and director of *Teen Encounter*, *Camp of the Nations* and *Wayside Maternity Home* for unwed mothers. He also directed the project of preparing curriculum for *World-Wide Bible Institutes*, which organizes Bible institutes in local churches and mission stations around the world. During this time he received his Doctorate (DD), from Toledo Bible College & Seminary.

Dr Shade has served for nineteen years with *Source of Light Ministries International*, eight years as General Director. He now serves as Director of Advanced Biblical Studies Department which administers both the *WWBI* program and *Ezra Institute*. Ruby has served along with her husband in every place and project. The Shades continue actively serving with SLM in Bible teaching, evangelism and conference ministry both in this country and abroad.

BY THE SAME AUTHOR:

The Prophetic Destiny of Israel & The Islamic Nations could hardly be more timely. How is the present conflict going to end? What will happen to Israel? -- To Islam? This book finds the biblical answers to those questions and more.

* * * * *

Amazed by Grace, the book that tells of God's marvelous faithfulness and miraculous acts in the life and ministry of Dr. Bill & Ruby Shade, is available in bookstores and on Amazon now.

Order your copy at:
BillShade.org

Dispensational Chart:

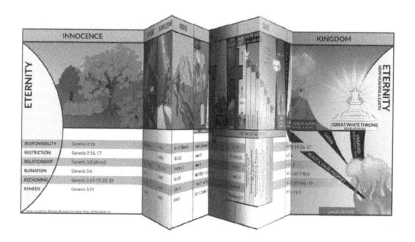

This beautifully illustrated, full-color Dispensational Chart makes an excellent reference or study aid to accompany this book. The Dispensational Chart is available in several formats that will make a valuable addition to any study library.

Order your copy at:
BillShade.org